Three Churches: One Spirit

THREE CHURCHES:
ONE SPIRIT

JAMES F. GRAVES
DELOS L. SHARPTON
LEWIS C. LAMPLEY

BROADMAN PRESS
Nashville, Tennessee

© Copyright 1978 • Broadman Press
All rights reserved.

4263-09

ISBN: 0-8054-6309-7

Dewey Decimal Classification: 286
Subject heading: CHRISTIAN SOCIAL MINISTRIES
Library of Congress Catalog Card Number: 77-81205
Printed in the United States of America.

Preface

A luncheon meeting called by a concerned young pastor issued in a most exciting mission venture. Delos Sharpton, then pastor of Southside Baptist Church in Saint Petersburg, Florida, had invited Jim Graves, pastor of First Baptist Church in the same city, to meet with him to share some concerns about the church he served. Bill Guess, director of missions for Pinellas Baptist Association, was invited to share in the discussion. The concerns had to do with the deterioration of the Southside Baptist Church due to its location in a transitional neighborhood. The outgrowth of the conversation that day was a dream which would involve a three-way merger of Southside and First Baptist churches and a third church, the Tabernacle Baptist Church.

The pastor of the Tabernacle Baptist Church, Lewis Lampley, was contacted concerning his interest in the proposal. Tabernacle Baptist Church was a black Baptist fellowship which had only recently been received into the Pinellas Baptist Association. Upon the expression of interest by leaders in Tabernacle Church, efforts began to effect the realization of the dream.

This book is the detailed unfolding of those efforts which consummated in September, 1975, with the constitution of the Southside Tabernacle Baptist Church. Each pastor takes a turn in telling the story at each stage. Chapter one is written by Graves, chapter two by Sharpton, and chapter three by Lampley. The cycle repeats, with chapter four by Graves, and so on. Finally, Graves has contributed the epilogue.

Contents

ONE

The Inner City

To understand a church, you have to know something about its location. First Baptist Church of Saint Petersburg, Florida, is in the old, established central business district. The usual term for such an area today is "inner city."

The inner city of Saint Petersburg saw the slow deterioration so common to cities in the fifties and sixties. Now, in the mid-seventies, our city is trying to see and deal with its real problems. It seeks to experience revitalization.

Among these problems is the exodus of much retail business to outlying shopping centers. One of the very first shopping centers in the nation was Central Plaza, at Thirty-fourth Street and Central Avenue in Saint Petersburg. This concentration of retail stores combined abundant parking, attractive new facilities, and convenient location. It was the first step in the gradual shift of the retail market away from downtown.

After Central Plaza was well established, other small centers began to spring up throughout the city. Then came the establishment of Tyrone Mall in 1972. Tyrone Mall became a new center of retail activity and further minimized the downtown business district. In land plan proposals now under consideration, Tyrone Mall and surrounding businesses are firmly considered a major activity center for years to come.

Not only was it difficult to compete with the new buildings and modern methods of the shopping centers, but the centers exposed a serious parking shortage downtown. The downtown business district was established when there was much more dependence on public transportation. Also at the time of the evolving of the central business district, one could hardly have forecast the amazing multiplication of automobile traffic. Consequently, Saint Petersburg, as many cities in our land, did not incorporate large parking lots in the development of the downtown retail market center. For many years this was not a serious problem. When the shopping centers began to emerge in convenient locations around the city, they capitalized on the lack of parking downtown by building large, well-lighted parking lots surrounding the retail stores.

With the success of so many outlying shopping facilities, stores in the downtown business district often found it necessary to close or relocate. Typically, these stores would experience a rather slow decline before facing the reality of the situation and dealing with their problems. Through the last fifteen years or so there has been an increasing problem in the downtown of vacant stores with unattractive store fronts, manifesting decline. Such deterioration often has a contagious effect and Saint Petersburg was not immune to the problem.

The reality of inner city blight is actually the spread of the very phenomena described in the flight to the suburbs. Fortunately, even with the classic signs of inner city decay at work, Saint Petersburg was able to avoid the level of decline of many such cities. In no small measure this is attributable to two very strong retail centers yet functioning in downtown effectively. The Maas Brothers and Webb's City enterprises still show signs of lively activity and modern marketing.

Corresponding to the shift of the retail centers to the outlying shopping centers, another factor was at work. For many years Saint Petersburg had been known as a beautiful city for the older person to come for rest and relaxation during the cold winter months. Through the years many of the people who came and enjoyed the warm sunshine and friendly acceptance of the city, returned upon their retirement from business to make the suncoast city their retirement home. A quarter of a century ago most of the winter visitors who came to Saint Petersburg were affluent. The old hotels in the city reflect the prosperity of the "boom" years. The economy of the city thrived then with the influx of visitors who were willing to pay for a good time in the sun with the many conveniences the city provided.

A very subtle shift occurred through the last twenty-five years. Little by little the affluent visitor from the north was attracted to other locations with more conveniences and brighter lights. Those who had come to St. Petersburg through the boom years continued to come out of fondness for the city, but as they died, there were no new families being attracted to take their places. No new hotels comparable to the magnificent facilities of yesteryear were built, and there were less and less accommodations that would appeal to the fewer and fewer affluent visitors that would come. Consequently, with the passing years there was a shift in the buying power potential of the winter visitor who came to the city. Many residents and businesses were very reluctant to accept the reality of economic decline associated with the change in winter guests.

Recent marketing studies in Saint Petersburg have pointed out a corresponding problem. Many, if not most, of the guest accommodations in Saint Petersburg were built fifty or sixty years ago. Many lovely old homes and hotels that speak of a grace and elegance of the past have gradually been converted into rooming houses for both the permanent resident and the winter visitor. With the inevitable decline of the years and the subtle shift in financial potential of the winter visitor, these rooming houses have found it increasingly difficult to modernize their facilities. In turn, these small businesses have found it even more difficult to make ends meet economically.

With this gradual decline in housing accommodations downtown, more and more residents on limited income were attracted to live in the inner city. While many affluent former visitors were still moving to the city to make it their retirement home, they were building beautiful homes on the waterfront or in other newer sections of the city. And, of course, the advent of the condominium drew most of the affluent permanent residents away from the older residential houses and hotels of downtown. The houses and the hotels downtown were divided into smaller and smaller apartments to accommodate the smaller budgets of the residents and the rising costs of the owners. Today, along with several beautiful apartment complexes and a number of beautiful homes in and near downtown, there is a predominance of older residents on somewhat limited incomes. Most of these are self-sustaining and maintain their pride and dignity, but they lack the financial resources to make the downtown area a thriving marketplace for retail businesses.

Interestingly, the growth of downtown as a residence for the older citizen on limited income has caused the city to avoid what many other cities have experienced in the developing ghettos. While the old hotels and homes of the inner city have not been able economically to modernize and replace their facilities, they have kept them attractively painted and appealing in appearance. Much of the grace of life a generation ago has been preserved and there is generally a comfortable life-style in evidence among the retirees who live downtown. In place of ethnic groups of poverty level who frequently inhabit the ghettos of abandoned apartments and retail businesses in other cities, Saint Petersburg has a large population of older white citizens on limited, but self-sufficient incomes.

While the distinction of the downtown resident as being perhaps lower middle-income, as opposed to poverty level, has probably slowed the exodus to the suburbs by the lower middle class, as is typical of other cities, it nonetheless has caused some serious economic problems. If the businesses cater to the limited income of the downtown resident, they will not market in such a manner as to attract the outlying residents to make the trip into the inner city to shop. Without the trade from the residents in a larger context of the city the businesses cannot exist. So their dilemma is a serious one as they seek to maintain a viable economic life downtown.

The economic realities confronted by the downtown businesses issue in certain very real problems for the city in general. Through the years, the downtown business district in Saint Petersburg, as in other cities, has provided the tax base for the financial stability of the city. Along with all of the other problems faced by downtown businesses that have caused many to move to the suburbs, the joint problems of high land cost and high taxes have compounded their problems. The city needs a strong downtown because of the tax base it has always maintained for the many improvements desired and needed by the residents.

Another of the rather typical problems faced by Saint Petersburg through the last quarter of a century or so, has been the effects of transportion. As has already been noted, the city was planned and was evolving in a time when one could hardly prophesy the tremendous influx of the automobile. Fortunately, early planners in the city demanded wide streets and an orderly organization of traffic so that modern traffic is routed for maximum efficiency and safety.

The unavailability of parking is a problem faced by the retail establishments, the office complexes, hotels, governmental centers, churches, and every other entity downtown. Due to the lack of necessity for such facilities in the days when the city was coming into shape, few provisions were made. Now due to the high cost of land in the central business district, as well as the tax structure and the limitation of retail traffic, the lack of parking is a serious deterrent to attempts to take the kinds of action necessary to effect some revitalization.

When fewer individuals had their own transportation, public transportation made the downtown the center of activity. Now, the ready availability of personal modes of transportation make the suburbs more accessible and attractive. Though the buses operated by the city still focus traffic to the downtown area as the transfer point to most other locations, the rather limited use does not bring many people downtown as public transportation once did.

Saint Petersburg has many very positive aspects that have kept the above mentioned problems from depressing all efforts toward vital existence. The waterfront area, known as the bayfront, is one of the most appealing and beautiful places to be found anywhere. Recognized as one of the city's most favorable features, the bayfront has been the focus of much investment toward the future. Wisely, the city set out years ago to purchase as much waterfront land as possible to preserve for parks and green space.

Along with an attractive park running along the bayfront in the heart of the downtown district, the city has maintained a very fine public swimming beach. It has built a modern structure at the end of a public pier with a restaurant and other features for the enjoyment of residents and visitors alike. A most adequate coliseum and auditorium have been erected on the waterfront to attract many interesting entertainment and cultural activities for the people of the city. A very fine baseball stadium has been erected for the spring training of the Saint Louis Cardinals and the New York Mets.

While the retail businesses have been migrating to the suburbs, financial institutions have been building better and larger facilities in the downtown area. Modern and attractive facilities of strong banks and savings and loan organizations give the downtown a stable appearance and a firm commitment to the future. The total deposits of these institutions establish downtown Saint Petersburg as a financial center of the city and the county.

An excellent arts museum is located in the park area near the waterfront. The very fine collections and activities of the museum offer the downtown a cultural distinction. Other cultural ac-

James F. Graves

tivities reflect a vitality and a quality of life that still characterize Saint Petersburg as a lovely place to live.

Downtown Saint Petersburg has a number of strategic government offices and activities. There is a concentration of city management offices in the inner city which brings a number of people downtown and contributes much to the stability of the area. A county office building and a state office complex adjacent to the city hall join to make up what is referred to as the government complex. A federal office building some blocks away affords easy access for downtown residents in need of assistance and at the same time offers employment to a number of residents.

Added to these government offices are a number of office buildings developed by the private sector and rented to a myriad of professionals and business functions. Recent marketing studies developed by professional consultants for the city of Saint Petersburg indicate that the emphasis of the future for the city will be in the increasing demand for office space in the downtown area as opposed to retail establishments.

A number of old, established churches add solidarity downtown and contribute to the cultural stability of the entire area. No less than six major churches are within two blocks of the goverment complex around city hall. These churches have long ministered to the number of people who come as visitors in the winter as well as to the permanent residents who have found Saint Petersburg a wonderful place to live.

The University of South Florida, which has its main campus in Tampa, has an established branch campus in downtown Saint Petersburg. For some years this extension has attracted a number of commuters to classes primarily in the evenings. The Florida Board of Regents decided in 1975 to enlarge the Saint Petersburg campus. Land is being purchased and initial stages of construction are underway. The estimates for the future indicate some 17,500 students will be attending the Saint Petersburg campus within ten years. Many of these students will continue to be commuters, but plans are under way for housing and other supportive services for those who will live in the downtown area. This development holds the promise of new vitality for downtown Saint Petersburg.

Positive factors are at work for the revitalization of downtown in Saint Petersburg. Work on Interstate 275 through the heart of the city has been about half completed. Construction is well under way on two feeder corridors that will bring traffic downtown on Fifth Avenue North and Fifth Avenue South which will embrace the central business district. The anticipation of this transportation aid, and its approaching completion, has engendered much enthusiasm among those trying to maintain a vital downtown district. The city of Saint Petersburg has effected a number of improvements in public facilities in downtown and is making substantial investment in securing the viability of the inner city. Considerable effort by the private sector of the community is committed to the constant improvement of the central business district. I serve as chairman of the Downtown Improvement Authority, responsible to the city council, and charged with the task of plans and actions which will contribute to the development of the downtown district.

With the problems of downtown and the positive factors at work in the city for the revitalization of the downtown area, it would not seem strange for businesses and even churches to be absorbed in their own problems to the extent that they would not be aware, let alone involved, in the problems of those in the outlying areas.

TWO

A Transitional Suburb

The south side of Saint Petersburg was a potentially rapid growing suburban development when Southside Baptist Church was organized in 1934. This potential for growth was actualized in the years that followed. New families moving to Saint Petersburg were attracted to the neighborhood surrounding Southside Baptist Church. This trend continued for nearly forty years. By the late fifties and early sixties progress of the neighborhood began to wane. The community around Southside Baptist Church started to regress in its attractiveness and appeal. The community began a slow transition from a white community to a black community.

When Southside Baptist Church was organized forty-five years ago, the community had a great deal of sameness. The people were about the same age, the same educational attainment, the same economic status, and the same race, white. The community that once had so much sameness, became a thing of the past. By 1975, the community was a hodgepodge of age, race, economic, and educational attainment.

The struggle for identity and survival on the part of Southside Church was occasioned by the crisis of community in transition. The coming of blacks had caused the exodus of whites from the community. The whites remaining in the community were mostly elderly, unable at this juncture in their lives to make the transition to another section of the city. The transition in the community was not only racial but economic and social. The value of the properties in the community, including the church property, decreased in value as the influx of blacks and whites of a lower economic status increased. The sameness of the community that once produced a social closeness among neighbors was replaced by suspicion and distrust.

The geographic community surrounding Southside Baptist Church in 1975 was made up of middle and lower income blacks and whites. The racial distribution was about 70 to 80 percent black and 30 to 20 percent white. The following information from the Pinellas County Census Tracts gives a good picture of the community. The median family income of families in the community around Southside Baptist Church was $4,143. The median school years completed was under ten years. The population under eighteen years of age was 40 to 49 percent. The median residential value was $7,800. The median rent was $70.00. The south side of Saint Petersburg according to the 1970 Census Tracts showed an 11 percent decrease in the population. This was due to the influx of blacks and the exodus of whites from the community.

Southside Church was dealing with a changing community, one changing from white to black. There seemed to be a lack of desire on the part of the community to be a part of Southside Baptist Church, even if they were welcomed. The scene had changed since the early sixties. The black community seemingly did not want to be a part of the white establishment. Even if the door was open, they did not want to enter. This coupled with the lack of resources at Southside Baptist Church made ministering most difficult. The question Southside Church faced was what to do to ensure that the mission of Jesus Christ was carried on in its neighborhood. Southside Baptist Church had gone from aggressive outreach to survival. Now the church was called on to examine its position in relationship to its changing community.

THREE

The Black Reality

Few things on God's earth are as real—as permanent—as the state of blackness. The cloak of color or race can be worn cheerfully like a bright, attractive garment, or it can be borne grudgingly like the proverbial albatross. The manner in which he handles the reality of blackness is left to each man's discretion.

Freedom of choice in the matter allows the spirit of color to wallow in self-pity, lamenting God's choice of race, or it allows the spirit to soar—to seek loftier heights, reveling in the Master's decision.

My own spirit was indeed soaring that fateful day when I, Lewis Charles Lampley, black Baptist minister, brought good tidings from our white brethren to the congregation of my own medium-sized church.

The whites were interested in a merger; how about us? Were we ready to help prove that integrated Christianity could and would work? Were we willing and able to meet the challenge of change . . . . the challenge of obliterating the centuries-old taboos which have kept blacks and whites from worshiping the same God under the same roof?

It was a fascinating thought, a timely thought!

The thought-provoking idea had been broached by two white ministers, Dr. James Graves and Rev. Delos Sharpton. Graves was (and is) pastor of First Baptist Church in downtown Saint Petersburg, and at the time Sharpton was pastor of Southside Baptist. We all were members of the Pinellas Baptist Association.

The discussion went like this: Each church had something the other needed. Tabernacle needed the room for expansion that Southside could offer, and Tabernacle had the members and vitality that Southside lacked. First Baptist also seemed to need new spiritual direction. Suppose Tabernacle's congregation moved to Southside, with the white members remaining or going to First Baptist, as their consciences dictated. Sharpton would join Graves as an assistant, and First Baptist would assume the debt liability for Southside (approximately $66,000), leaving the newly merged body unencumbered by debt.

The idea, admittedly approached cautiously by me at first, began to expand in my mind. Throughout the rest of the discussion and waiting period, I could actually feel the expansion taking place. The possibilities were mind-boggling!

We, the three ministers involved, didn't delude ourselves. We didn't view the merger as "realization of a long nurtured dream." We were, I like to believe, practical enough to view it, purely and simply, as an outgrowth of crisis.

The die was cast; I was guided by the Holy Spirit to relay the proposal to my flock. Not surprisingly, the idea was met with the usual "hows and whys"—the usual search for "hidden meanings" in dealings with white people. Tabernacle's officers and members were careful in their scrutiny of merger plans.

Were the whites sincere in the offer? Did they really want to make this thing work on a man-to-man basis, rather than servant-master basis? Could, indeed, they be trusted?

We ended that first meeting with prayer for divine direction. Our answer was soon forthcoming and the merger was effected to mutual satisfaction.

As pastor of the "integrated" congregation, I'm happy to report—it's working!

Perhaps ten years ago it would not have worked. As a matter of fact, as a young pastor, I received some disturbing counsel. . . . It came from a well respected and conscientious black deacon. He said, "Reverend, you are a good Bible teacher, but you cannot indoctrinate black people." My silent reply was, "We shall see!"

That deacon reflected the mentality of a great number of people who have a distorted view of biblical Christianity, scarred by racial prejudice. He also verbalized the problem of limited opportunity, and highlighted the struggle for a meaningful identity.

In reality though, there are *grounds for pessimism*.

Since days immemorial, black people have been despised, discriminated against, and exploited. The prevalence of a warped mind-set, even in an enlightened America, was permanently established by the framers of our national Constitution, when they viewed a segment of American citizens as only being chattel: "An item of tangible property other than real estate."—The New Merriam Webster Pocket Dictionary

Is there any wonder then that it is "almost impossible" for ethnic majorities to see and accept ethnic minorities as equals?

The false sense of superiority has given occasion for some of the following rationalizations:

Black people or 'they' will be better off with their own kind.

They are nice people but I don't think that God intended . . . .

How would you like for your daughter or son to marry one?

We don't understand them, and they don't understand us.

I have been exposed to that kind of verbosity and rationalism more times than I care to mention.

Killjoy is not my object here, but it is astounding as we take a look at many major corporations, most of the major sports, and industry that any intellectually honest person has to agree that minorities have been great contributors to the making of America.

It is amazing and incredible, but as true as can be, America has developed by the efforts of us all, and that means you and me.

What about the kingdom from a black's point of view. Questions arise. Remember the European and American image of Christianity. Tenets and teachings are characterized by "whiteness," instead of righteous acts. The educated as well as the uneducated person in the black community has a hard time understanding how the same people who worship in an all white congregation, can claim to love and serve a just God, and participate in unjust dealings on a day-to-day basis. So the questioning goes, If God is on the white man's side, then is he against us?

Such views are not held by me. But I have to spend a great deal of time helping my people understand the actions, reactions, and responses of many white Christians, not just white people per se, but Christian people.

The most undisputed argument is "The most segregated hour of the week is eleven o'clock Sunday morning." Many of the accusers are not interested in anybody's worship service. The point being made is "Your God, evidently cannot change the 'man,' so what can he do for me?" Many blacks contend, "Christianity is the white man's tool to keep the black man under subjection."

The abrasive interrogation of some is even more raucous. They ask black believers, "What has Jesus done for you, educationally, economically, and politically?"

In the past, we did not have adequate answers, but in recent days God has been raising up an army of young articulate black believers in minority communities who have ready answers. Hope is raised as many hearts have thrilled when these words of M. S. Rice were recited:

> It is amazing and incredible
> But true as it can be,
> God loves and understands us all:
> And that means you and me.
> His grace is all sufficient
> For both the young and old

For the lonely and the timid,
For the brash and for the bold.
And no matter what your past has been,
Trust God to understand.
And no matter what your problem is,
Just put it in his hand.
For in all of our unloveliness,
This great God loves us still,
He loved us since the world began
And what's more he always will.

The words of that poem characterize the distilled essence of the gospel message that many of us in the black community have responded to.

Church buildings were the most valuable pieces of property in our communities for many years. The sanctuaries and fellowship halls were the centers of our cultural molding, and religious life. At least once a month and each summer during a week-long revival we heard that, "you must be born again." In many quarters, this message came from self-educated theologians, who had been ignored by their counterparts, and sometimes barred from Bible institutes, Bible colleges, and evangelical seminaries. Still, those stalwarts were able to inspire their listeners to look for a "bright side somewhere."

The joy-sorrow hymns and spirituals were the basis for "running-on to see what the end will be." But the generation of the late thirties and early forties was not interested in "pie in the sky" after awhile. They wanted "some ham and eggs now."

In the late fifties and early sixties, we were coming of age. And then, serendipity! That is, unexpected discoveries of lucid gospel messages that could not be kept from across the railroad tracks because radio and television ministries directed by evangelists and pastors brought the gospel into our homes. Our hearts were strangely warmed and challenged by these men—many of them, too, were victims of racism and sectionalized evangelism. But on radio, they faithfully proclaimed a gospel that was difficult for them to practice. During this same era, God began to use movements like Intervarsity fellowship, the Navigators, Tom Skinner Associates, and Campus Crusade for Christ to reach college and university students. These associations were able to bring some balance to the ministry of the less prepared men as well as those who had attended liberal seminaries.

The atmosphere in the black community produced two types of congregations, the emotional and the classical. The emotional congregation ranges from mild to extreme emotionalism and the classical from moderate to ultraformal. Both groups have many good programs, but isolation has brought about an "ingrown" and "aquarium" mentality which has a commitment to sameness. This commitment says that there is something unique about us and we intend to keep it that way.

But the young, black evangelical has a commitment to an aggressive, balanced ministry, one that takes us to the marketplaces, and many other strata of our urban world.

As ethnic minorities, we are not discouraged or dismayed, but rather enthusiastic about the role that has been entrusted to us and hasten to say yes to the question raised by the apostle James: "Hearken, my beloved brethren, Hath not God chosen the poor of this world rich in faith, and heirs of the kingdom which he hath promised to them that love him?" (Jas. 2:5).

The words of Deuteronomy 7:7 refer primarily to the nation of Israel, but they are also appropriate to illustrate how God can use any oppressed people to flush out the concept of love depicted by the words of Eddie Cantor: "Love isn't like a reservoir; you'll never drain it dry. It's much more like a natural spring. The longer and further it flows, the stronger and the deeper and the clearer it becomes."

When I became pastor, racial tension was almost chronic in this country. As I reminisce, it is interesting to see that God was at work during those days of racial unrest and civil disorder. Kennedy's new frontier and Johnson's great society offered hope for many disfranchised people, but many of those hopes were dashed as an insensitive administration was ushered in on a national level. Again, an ominous cloud settled over blacks. The power structure and Satan meant it for evil, but God turned it into eternal good for many. Many people, and particularly black people, turned to God as a result of the perplexing frustrations.

This turning to God was mostly through a process of elimination, because nothing else had worked or promised lasting and fulfilling values. I stand amazed with Paul when he said: "O the depth of the riches both of the wisdom and knowledge of God! how unsearchable are his judgments, and his ways past finding out! For of him, and through him, and to him are all things; to whom be glory forever" (Rom. 11:33,36).

America will never be the same because of the spiritual renaissance that is taking place in the black community on a small but effective scale. "The kingdom of God does not exist because of your efforts or mine. It exists because God reigns. Our part is to enter this kingdom and bring our life under his sovereign will" (T. Z. Koo).

The black reality is restricted by limited opportunities, racial prejudice, and an identity crisis. In spite of these restrictions, blacks are being used by God in a growing capacity today.

To give the reader a fuller picture of black life, let me share some of my own experiences.

Frolicking over the rolling Alabama farmland of my home . . . sitting straight-backed in the little Baptist church where my family belonged . . . these things are among my earliest—and fondest memories.

The time of my childhood was that bleak period in American history known as "The Panic." The Great Depression had scarcely slackened its strong hold on the country when I came on the scene. The morals and economy of the nation were tottering

Delos F. Sharpton

on new ground—ground turned by President Franklin D. Roosevelt.

I'm told I made a somewhat noisy entrance into the world in the wee hours of May 16, 1937, with the assistance of Mrs. Luella Knox, the neighborhood "granny lady." My birthplace carries the picturesque name of Pineywoods. It nestles between two small Alabama towns, Tennille and Brundidge, in Pike County.

The word bittersweet always comes to mind when I think of my childhood. The sweetness, as for most black children, was based on the security of belonging . . . of being a part of a family unit, a church unit, a community unit. The bitterness was fostered by a sense of hopelessness for a little black boy growing up in the cruel Alabama hills.

I don't remember exactly when I first realized the importance of an education—and how slim were my chances of getting one.

My parents were of a generation in which few blacks had gone beyond the third grade. Blacks living in their vicinity, I mean. Blacks in their particular age group sort of scoffed at education, labeling book-larnin' "foolishness." This was particularly applicable when it came to educating black boys; "Why send a boy to school when all he's going to do anyhow is plow a mule?" What little school-going that was done in our settlement was done by the girls.

I did, however, manage to attend school several months each term. I went regularly from the first through the third grades. Then I was big enough to work in the fields. From then on, until I got through the eighth grade, I only went to school about four months a school term—after all the farm work was done. There were eight children in my family and the pattern was the same for all the boys.

No situation, though, is all bad. I remember vividly the fun we had trudging to the little schoolhouse—wading through streams, walking half-submerged logs, chasing each other through the woods. Oh, yes, there were school buses in our area—but not for black children!

Ironic, isn't it, how the kids and parents today are sending up such howls about busing, when we would have welcomed escape from the icy ground and winds within the confines of a warm, dry school bus!

It was rare at that time to find a black boy or girl in the Pineywoods area who had completed, or even attended, high school. It was almost unheard of for a black youngster in our neck-of-the-woods to have attended college.

Although I had never ventured farther away from home than Tennille and Brundidge, I *knew* deep in my heart that there was something more to life than the rolling acres of cotton, corn, and peanuts, that I saw and worked in every day. I wasn't very old when I promised myself I would find out what lay beyond the hills. There had to be more to life than gettin' up, hitchin' up, gatherin' up, and settlin' up. I was determined not to grow up to work all year, then have Mr. Charlie tell me "ya 'et it up" when it was time to get my share.

My determination to escape sharecropping was strengthened by all the plowing and picking and hoeing. Then, wonder of wonders, I met a man who showed a genuine interest in me and my future. He was Mr. Witt—dear, wise old Mr. Witt, our principal at Pea River Elementary and Junior High School. Ignoring the fact that the all-black school was understaffed, un-accredited, un-everything, Mr. Witt did his best to encourage the children to apply themselves and take advantage of whatever was offered. He urged us on with a rather shopworn motto: "Be the labor great or small, do it well—or not at all!" I adopted the motto as my own and have applied it over and over through the years.

Although the future was still foggy in my mind, I vowed that I would be "the best." "Great," said a small voice within me, adding, "but the best *what?*" Clear direction still eluded me.

While I was in the tenth grade, a career consultant visited our school. He asked the inevitable question of each class member: "And what do *you* want to be when you grow up?" My classmates roared with laughter when I answered, "I'm going to be a jet pilot!" For months I was angry with them for laughing, although I did realize the humor of my answer; the closest I had ever been to a jet airplane was when one flew over our fields—umpteen miles up in the clouds.

I later decided to become a barber. The decision served me well. I passed the examinations, received my license, and worked as a barber twelve years after moving to Saint Petersburg.

Another important note was sounded in my life during the 1950's. I married my childhood sweetheart, Geraldine Meadows. We were wed in 1956, and moved to the Suncoast the same year. We have seven children, two of whom are students at Florida A and M University in Tallahassee, and another at West Point Military Academy in upstate New York. And although I never did get to fly a jet, I have been privileged to fly thousands of miles on jet aircraft. More about that later . . .

My first religious experience occurred when I was eight. I joined the aforementioned Baptist church, and was genuinely surprised that I didn't feel much different after baptism than I did before.

Even though I didn't fully understand what being a Christian meant or involved, I knew I wanted to go to heaven and not "the other place"—just in case I happened to die!

It was during the winter of 1962 that I actually was saved . . . that God took my life into his hands. My rebirth took place as I listened to a radio religious program conducted by an evangelist, Oliver B. Green. He concluded his sermon that Friday with this invitational prayer: "God, be merciful to me, a sinner. I am so sorry for my sins—please forgive me. Right now, I am inviting your Son, Jesus Christ, to come into my life . . . . Lord Jesus, come into my life, and save me. I receive you as my Savior and Lord. Thank you for saving me." I repeated those words after

Evangelist Green, and heaven came down and glory filled my soul. For me, it was a definite turning point. Since that day, life has been an adventure, a pilgrimage.

Knowing that God intended using me in the future, I was more than ever determined to prepare myself educationally. I completed high school at twenty-nine, and at thirty-five I earned the Bachelor of Religious Education degree from Florida Beacon College, Largo, Florida. I have done additional study in the field of theology at Florida Seminary, Lakeland, and Moody Bible Institute, Chicago. At present, I am involved in earning the Master's Degree in theology at Luther Rice Seminary, Jacksonville, Florida.

Since assuming the Tabernacle pastorate, I have been fortunate to travel to eight foreign countries on a thirty-day tour, and have attended sessions of the Baptist World Alliance in Tokyo, Japan, and this country.

For two years, I was an associate staff member for Campus Crusade for Christ, and participated in management conferences for that organization. I am a member of the local minister's groups, the Florida chapter of the National Evangelical Association, the Sickle Cell Anemia Foundation, and the National Association for the Advancement of Colored People (NAACP).

FOUR

First Baptist Church

During the decade of the sixties and early into the seventies, First Baptist Church showed signs of problems not dissimilar to those of the city in which it lived and functioned. As is so often true, the church faced problems parallel to those of the city, and only in an understanding of those problems can one understand the subtle changes that occurred in the church.

Compare the move of retail businesses to the suburbs. Newer and more modern facilities were available, greater accessibility and convenience were experienced, and an abundance of free parking made shopping easier. More and more, churches erected in the suburbs were attracting people living nearby. Through the decade of the fifties, First Baptist Church, just as many other old downtown churches across the country, sponsored and helped a number of churches to be established in the outlying areas of Saint Petersburg.

For a time, the struggling smaller congregations could not afford to call the better trained and experienced pastors, and neither could they afford a professional staff of ministers to help guide the program of the church. Consequently, even as these churches began to grow the downtown church maintained its strong appeal as the church with strong preaching, the finest music program, and the best all-round program for the entire family. As time moved on and these churches attracted more and more people, they secured strong staff personnel and built well balanced programs of activity. The suburban churches offered an attractive alternative to some of the problems of going to the downtown church.

First Baptist Church, at the same time, was experiencing other very typical problems. Retail establishments found it difficult to compete with suburban centers which offered plenty of free parking and so did First Baptist Church. Owning only one very small parking lot which would take about a dozen cars, the church faced a negative reaction from many of its longtime members. They found it increasingly attractive to stay in the neighborhood where they lived to attend church on Sunday. To a greater extent, new residents in the city would drive by the downtown location. Seeing no parking lots, they would assume it would be a problem to try to park on Sunday and would choose another church, often without even visiting the church.

The parking dilemma of First Baptist was, and is, as much psychological as practical. Two of the financial institutions which have been mentioned as having enlarged and enhanced their facilities downtown, have made available to the church their parking buildings on Sunday. One of the well established retail stores nearby has opened its parking garage for use by church members attending services on Sunday. A half block away are two municipal lots which, though quite small, are very convenient. A small lot owned by a nearby hotel is available on some occasions. All of these parking facilities are used to some extent by four other large downtown churches as well as First Baptist Church. Nonetheless, there are empty parking spaces on practically every occasion, but they are not the highly visible spaces so attractive on a parking lot typical of a suburban church or shopping center.

For residents accustomed to the very convenient and accessible parking of the suburb, the lack of visible and available parking is a distraction. In addition, when they drive by and see the number of churches claiming the minimum number of spaces available, it is a natural assumption that parking would be too great a problem to cope with in order to attend a downtown church. In the respect that more spaces are available than appears, the problem is largely psychological. However, a very real problem exists in seeking to accommodate weekday activities in the church when the financial institutions and the retail businesses are utilizing their parking facilities to the maximum.

The change in the pattern of transportation also takes its toll on a downtown church. Once the necessity of public transportation made downtown the center of activity in the city. With the advent of readily available personal transportation, downtown lost its distinction as the activity center; and that, in itself, attracted many to shop and to worship in other locales. First Baptist Church, along with many other downtown churches, began to see its place of distinction erode.

Another of the parallel problems of the church with the city was that of deterioration in facilities. When I visited with the pulpit committee and viewed the facilities, a factor which was at once a disappointment and a challenge was the need of the buildings for maintenance and redecoration. One of the members of the pulpit committee had been reared in the community and had attended the church from the time he was a small boy. He indicated that later he went back through the buildings and tried to put himself in the situation of someone visiting the buildings for the first time. He expressed amazement at what he saw on that tour. Now, instead of being stimulated to the memory of great experiences he could recall, he saw paint that was peeling. Places needed cleaning, and there was a general need for work to restore the brightness and attractiveness of the church plant. He had realized what is difficult oftentimes for someone who has attended a church for a long time to realize. A newcomer sees the facilities without the good memories of past experiences. The state of repair of the buildings speak of the aggressiveness of the people to attract new people to the fellowship—or the lack of it. Just as deteriorating store fronts in a downtown are catalytic to further decline, so when the church plant fails to project a vitality and beauty, one problem brings on another.

Another problem of St. Petersburg in particular which had effect on the problems of First Baptist Church, had to do with the subtle change in the nature of the winter visitor. To hear former staff members and longtime members tell of the experiences of a couple of decades ago is enough to make one long for the good old days. For in those times the visitors to Saint Petersburg and First Baptist Church would number some of the most distinguished citizens of the nation. It was a thrill and a challenge to the church to minister to these people and the church enjoyed considerable prestige in this ministry. Apparently, at one time some of these visitors made substantial financial contributions to the church.

But, as the more affluent visitor frequented Saint Petersburg less and less, and as the number of winter visitors declined, the need of the ministry changed. This change in need was not easily recognized. When I first came to serve the church I was told that attention must be paid to the winter visitors, since they gave much to the church. Upon careful study, however, of the the giving record of the church, it was discovered that actually very little of the income of the church derived from these winter visitors. Moreover, the church had taken the shape of this ministry to a disproportionate extent. It was determined that for the church to have a future, more emphasis would have to be given to the permanent resident, but with no minimization of cordiality and welcome to the visitor.

With emphasis on the winter visitor and the retired citizen who may have first met the church as a winter visitor, the church faced a rising median age. From early in the sixties to early in the seventies the Sunday School attendance of children in grades one through six dropped from 19 percent of the total to about 12 percent of the total. A commitment was made to develop an effective ministry to the aging in our community, but at the same time to concentrate outreach on the young and middle adults. It was a strong conviction on the part of leadership that only as young adults were enlisted to be the church of tomorrow could there be a continuing ministry to senior adults.

To accomplish the ministry with senior adults, a pilot project was entered with the Home Mission Board to explore ways of ministering effectively to the older adult. Programs of Vacation Bible School, weekday continuing education, pleasure trips, and crafts of various kinds were developed and continue to function effectively. Efforts continue to develop which will enable the church to enlarge its outreach with young people and young families.

Each church must face the changing challenges with the passing of time. The decade of the seventies brought new kinds of opportunities and at the same time there was a passing of others. The church sought to minister to the needs of the community as they existed in the present. A program of teaching conversational English was initiated to help foreign-born individuals, particularly Cubans, function effectively in our city. That program of work gained enough strength to be of considerable assistance later with the influx of many Vietnamese and Laotian refugees to the area. The involvement in the lives of these people from other lands has given the members of First Baptist Church a deeper sense of ministry and meaning.

Another factor in the new character developing in the life of First Baptist had to do with a ministry to the deaf. A couple in the church, while attending Home Mission Week at Ridgecrest, became committed to helping deaf people. Neither of them had had any training or particular exposure to people with this need, but they came home determined to prepare themselves for this work. Their commitment has issued in a full ministry to the deaf through First Baptist Church which has reached a number of people with a touch of love in the name of Jesus. At the same time it has established in the fellowship of the church an interest for people with special needs.

While an interest and an involvement was developing in the

church toward helping people with special needs through such programs as the conversational English classes and the program for the deaf, a kind of introversion was occurring out of necessity. Having always had a strong commitment to the support of world missions through the Cooperative Program and mission offerings, the church continued its commitment to world missions. However, rather than think in terms of mission sites and extension in the county, the church began to face the reality of maintaining a vital ministry downtown. A number of priorities were recognized as necessary.

In addition to the commitment to emphasize outreach with the younger adults, the church leadership faced the necessity of increasing its financial base. For a number of years the church had fallen over a hundred thousand dollars short of its projected budget. Though the budget was increased year after year, the serious deficiency was not being narrowed. Because of the problem, at times more than 50 percent of the income of the church was being expended for salaries and another 20 percent for missions. The 20 to 30 percent left for the entire church program and improvement of facilities was inadequate to develop an aggressive program of work. In 1972, with a 26 percent increase in budget gifts, a 15 percent cut was effected in the budget.

In a span of five years the income of the church doubled largely through a program of stewardship education. Whereas, some dependence had always been felt upon a few residents and visitors of means, emphasis was placed upon the necessity of the involvement of every member in the financial responsibility of the church. This emphasis has not only served to increase the financial resources of the church but also to underscore the very real need for meaningful involvement of every church member.

In that same time frame, a reorganization in the staff which combined certain responsibilities enabled the church to increase the remuneration to the staff in proportion to the escalating cost of living increase and to cut the percentage of the total budget going to personnel. These factors combined to enable the church to enlarge its program budget and develop some new strategies for reaching people. To the credit of the church, at no time was there a serious consideration of reducing the contribution through the Cooperative Program for world mission support. Financial support has continued to grow each year through dollar increases even though the percentage has remained the same.

Another of the commitments of the church concerned the improvement of the facilities. Of major concern was the worship center. An extensive program of renovation was accomplished with a firm that specialized in such work. The sanctuary was completely stripped of all furnishings, necessitating the church moving to an adjacent hotel for worship services for some seven weeks. When the project was completed, including the installation of a beautiful new fifty-two rank pipe organ, the church building had a new and inviting appearance. There was a new and exciting vitality added to the worship experiences as the worship center reflected the faith and hope of the people in the future of the church in God's grace. A part of the subconscious lack of confidence was dissipated and visitors were invited with a fresh enthusiasm.

The needs of other facilities claimed the attention of the church. The church offices had already been brightened up with paint, new carpets, and drapes. On the fifth floor of the educational building is a very fine outdoor recreational area. It is caged in with screening to protect the ones who utilize the area and to contain the basketballs and other equipment in use. The caging had become so rusted and insecure that very little use was being made of the facility. A complete restoration of the area was accomplished, making it not only safe but very appealing and colorful. Its use increased immediately. The halls and entrance ways were painted with tasteful colors changing from the institutional neutrality that had characterized the building.

The next area of concern was the nursery suite. These rooms

Lewis C. Lampley

were completely redecorated and carpeted with an emphasis on making them appealing to the young couples the church wanted to reach. New equipment was added to increase the teaching capabilities as well as the enjoyment of the children.

The renovation was successfully accomplished for approximately five hundred thousand dollars. During the process of renovation some two hundred thousand dollars was raised and paid on the work, leaving the church with an indebtedness of three hundred thousand dollars. That indebtedness was for work that secured our present but, at the same time, tied up our future to some extent.

Already there had begun discussions among the leadership of the church concerning the challenge of purchasing the hotel adjacent to the church property. Not only would the hotel give space for future expansion and much needed parking space immediately, but would also give an opportunity for ministry through serving senior adults in a residential hotel. Conversations concerning the possibility of buying the hotel always had to deal with the reality of the indebtedness the church had. The challenge of the acquisition of more property seemed somewhat remote early in the seventies.

When the opportunity and challenge to participate in a merger with the Southside Baptist Church and Tabernacle Baptist Church was presented, it had to be faced in the light of all the struggle to stay alive and vital in a downtown ministry. The responsibilities of sharing in that venture had to be weighed against the debt the church owed for the renovation and the financial challenges of balancing the budget of the church. Yet, it was in the facing of that unexpected challenge that First Baptist Church discovered some of the answers to its own needs and direction for the future:

FIVE

Southside Baptist Church

Church in Transition

Southside Baptist Church was organized on the basis of St. Matthew, chapter sixteen, verses eighteen and nineteen: ". . . upon this rock I will build my church; and the gates of hell shall not prevail against it. And I will give unto thee the keys of the kingdom of heaven: and whatsoever thou shalt bind on earth shall be bound in heaven: and whatsoever thou shalt loose on earth shall be loosed in heaven." There was a deep commitment to the cause of Christ on the part of the charter members. Indeed, the Father blessed their efforts. Southside Church did come a long way from those early days of meeting in a rented store, with wooden boxes and packing crates as pews. In 1945, property was purchased and a new building was erected in 1946. An educational building was built in 1955-56. In 1960 some additional property adjacent to the church property was purchased. In 1966, some additonal property was attained and a mission was started. For some thirty years the church experienced strong growth, effective leadership, and a meaningful ministry. Its programs and organizations were productive. Its gifts to missions increased each year. The church showed gains in all areas of service. Its choir, women's organizations, and youth organizations were always active and involved. These organizations were the recipients of many awards within the framework of the Southern Baptist Convention. Some of the church's young people entered full-time Christian Service. Southside Baptist

Church was a church with a proud tradition.

In the early spring of 1963, the church was confronted with the reality that it was located in a community that was in transition. It was believed that blacks would not move into the neighborhood as quickly as they did. In that same year, a group of blacks inquired into the possibility of buying the Southside Baptist Church property. This happened at a time when the mere mention of integration spread panic among many people.

When the congregation learned of this inquiry, the rumor mills went into high gear and at full speed. The reaction of the people was mixed. Some were confused; others thought the church had no choice but to move; still others wanted the church to assume a wait-and-see posture. At the next business meeting, following the inquiry by the group of blacks, the matter was presented to the people as honestly and openly as possible. Discussion of the subject was lengthy, ranging from getting out and moving to a new location to a few who felt the church should remain in its present location and integrate the membership if it came to that point. Following the general discussion, a motion was made to ask the interested blacks to make an offer on the church property. This motion was passed by the congregation. The authorized representatives of the church contacted the black group as directed by the church, but they declined to make an offer. For many of the members of Southside Church, the issue over blacks in the neighborhood and the church was closed. This was not the end of the issue, however; it was the beginning. This affair in 1963 is an important event in the history of Southside Baptist Church, for it was the beginning of the crisis of transition. The issue was not settled; it was very much alive. Blacks were moving into the neighborhood, and the rumor of blacks buying the church lived on. This had its effect on prospective members and on those thinking of moving into the neighborhood.

The issue of transition was not the only issue that Southside was called on to deal with beginning in the sixties. In 1966, three years after the racial issue surfaced, the church voted to purchase some property for a mission site. This was most significant. For a church in a transitional community to almost triple its indebtedness is remarkable. Southside Church did, however, increase its indebtedness from thirty-six thousand dollars in 1963 to almost one hundred and five thousand dollars in 1966. This increase in the church's indebtedness would surface later and play a major role in the drama that was to unfold.

In the late sixties, the neighborhood surrounding Southside Church began to move from a predominantly white community to a predominantly black one. As this shift in the community occurred, the facts could no longer be denied; things were changing. Southside Church and its community that had a marked degree of sameness, witnessed the change. The area that had felt it would not be affected by blacks moving to the south side of the city were awakened out of its sleep.

As a product of the Southern Baptist Convention, Southside had geared its programs and ministries to reaching white middle-class America. Then Southside found itself in the midst of a changing neighborhood. The homes making up its community were no longer occupied by the white middle class but by blacks and whites of a lower economic and social level. It is difficult for us personally to face change, and it is difficult for a church to witness the transition of its community. The church's emphasis on missions had been in the past an activity in some distant place. But, as the community changed, the membership found itself called on to "be" God's missionaries.

Southside Church decided to stay in this transitional community and "be" God's missionaries. The church accepted black members and began busing in black children for Sunday School. Some of the membership left and joined other churches. Others tolerated what was happening because it was their church. Others saw a challenge to "do" missions, while still others waited to see what was going to happen. During this time, a period of about five years, a minority of the membership made an effort to reach their community. They thought it would be easier than it was. However, the people of the community did not respond as expected, and this became a source of discouragement and frustration. The small victories along the way made the effort worthwhile.

By 1974, it became clear to even the most indifferent members of Southside that things were not what they should be. During the transition of the community and church, it became more evident that the church sustained the loss of members, the loss of a sense of direction, and was approaching an economic crisis. These factors coupled with being without a pastor created a climate of uncertainty.

In September, 1974, my ministry at Southside Baptist Church began. The decision to move to Saint Petersburg was not an easy one. Florida was a new field, unknown to my family and me. On the surface there was not anything that would attract a person to Southside. One could see from examining past records, seeing the community, the physical church plant, the indebtedness, and the makeup of the membership that the task would be most difficult. In spite of what appeared on the surface, I was impressed with the commitment, dedication, and spirit of the pastor selection committee, along with this was a deep personal feeling that God was calling and I must respond.

I began my ministry at Southside by trying to stabilize some of the present ministries, Sunday School, and worship services, and by trying to restore hope to those who had lost hope. I began a study of urban ministry and the urban church in transition.

A constant companion during those early days of my ministry at Southside were seminary class notes on the church and the community. I examined what other churches in similar situations were doing; for example, the Columbia Drive Baptist Church in Decatur, Georgia. I conferred on many occasions with Mr. Bert Purvis, our associational Christian social ministries director. An in church survey was conducted to determine church and community needs. A program of pastoral visitation was set up to gain insight into attitudes and the spirit of the membership.

The studies conducted and the visits made were most revealing. There was a fear among the membership to such degree that many would not attend evening services. There was a fear of a black take over. There was a chasm between the white and black cultures. The main attitude toward blacks was one of tolerance. There was a lack of understanding of community missions among the membership. In addition to these factors there was the membership itself, consisting mainly of individuals over fifty years of age. The Southside Church did not have the constituency to minister in the manner that the community demanded. Another factor was an economic one. The financial resources were not available to meet the ministry needs.

Therefore, it became an issue of mission. The church is called to minister to the community where it is located. If it can't do that, then it must look for ways to provide that ministry. The church that doesn't minister to the needs of its community loses its power. For the church is the body of Christ, and the purpose of its existence is to continue the ministry of Christ. Its ultimate aim is the reconciliation of man to God, thus enabling man to be what he was created to be. The church must be conscious of the fact that it does not exist for its own sake but rather exists to be God's instrument of reconciliation. As pastor of Southside it was my opinion that our church was not fulfilling its mission to its geographical community.

When ministry is not being done by a church, what should the pastor do? As pastor of Southside Church I saw these courses open to me:

(1) Stabilize the present situation and work with "what's there." Refuse to accept the reality of a community in transition.

(2) Resign with or without a place to go.

(3) Examine the situation as objectively as possible, with re-

gard to the present and future mission of this church. The examination must have thought and prayer behind it.

Struggle and conflict are always involved when a pastor and church seek to be true to their mission. The struggle is even greater when the community in which it is to minister takes on racial and economic characteristics different from those of individuals making up the church. It is necessary for God's people to seek what God wants a church to be and do and not be motivated by personal wants, wishes, and desires.

Therefore, being led of God in this matter, I sought to lead Southside Baptist Church in an examination of its present and future with regard to its mission. As pastor of Southside Baptist Church, I had to lead our people to realize that we were in a crisis community. Before I could do that I had to believe it myself. Many times the pastor of a church which is in a transitional community will not admit the reality that his church is in transition. The first step in the examination of Southside Baptist Church came about by our realizing that we were in a crisis community. Our church like many others soon realized that we were not by ourselves. A 1974 study by the Home Mission Board of the Southern Baptist Convention, drawn from 5,543 metropolitan churches, found that nearly 18 percent or one thousand churches were in communities changing racially or economically. In this study prepared by the Home Mission Board various types of criteria were used to determine a community in crisis. A church may be facing one or more of these: racial transition, commercial transition, economic transition, housing transition, social transition, or industrial transition. If the community is making some significant change in one or more of these areas, it becomes a crisis for the church. On the basis of this study and report it was my conclusion that Southside Baptist Church was clearly a church involved in a crisis community. There was racial transition, social transition, and economic transition as well.

Further examination of this study prepared by the Home

Mission Board was most significant and most revealing in regard to where Southside Church was at this particular time in its history. Southside, as has been stated earlier, was located in an established neighborhood. The Home Mission Board study revealed that 60 percent of the churches in communities of crisis are located in established neighborhoods. The largest number of churches therefore in crisis communities are located in established neighborhoods very similar to the neighborhood of Southside Baptist Church. Twenty-five and one half percent of these churches facing communities in crisis are changing from white middle class to middle and lower class black. It is quite difficult for a church like Southside to change from a middle class outreach to a lower black and white outreach.

To further illustrate the place of Southside Baptist Church in the scheme of churches in crisis communities throughout the Southern Baptist Convention, some characteristics of churches in crisis communities are listed below:

Resident Membership—The resident membership of these churches run the scale in size. Each size within the Southern Baptist Convention was represented in crisis communities in 1974. Nine percent had memberships 1-99, 15 percent had memberships of 100-200, while 35.6 percent had memberships of 200-500. Southside Baptist Church's membership indicated it was in the highest percentage group.

Average Sunday School Attendance—Sixty-five percent of the churches in crisis communities had less than 200 in Sunday School average attendance. Southside Baptist Church's average for the last ten years was below 200.

Receipts, Giving, and Indebtedness—Fifty-one and seven tenths percent of the churches in crisis communities had receipts of less than fifty thousand dollars annually. In 1974, Southside had forty-one thousand dollars, falling within the group of churches characteristic of a crisis community. Churches in crisis communities face financial crisis month by month. This was the case at Southside where we were continuously running in the red. Fifty per cent of the churches in crisis communities had an indebtedness of seventy-five thousand dollars or less. In 1974, Southside's indebtedness was seventy thousand dollars, again clearly showing that Southside Church had characteristics of a church in a crisis community.

Baptisms—Twenty-seven and six tenths percent of the churches in crisis communities had twenty-five or more baptisms in 1974. In 1974, Southside had twenty-five baptisms, thus showing another characteristic of churches in crisis communities.

Letters and Other Additions—About the same trend follows in letters as in baptisms. Fifty-nine percent of these churches had one to twenty-four additions by letter. Southside Baptist Church was within this category.

From examining this study, I concluded that our church was very characteristic of a church in a crisis community. I attempted to take this a step further by examining the last ten years of Southside Baptist Church, 1964-74.

Membership—Total membership in 1964 was 527. Total membership in 1974 was 337. The breakdown of the membership was even more revealing. Keep in mind that our church was a church community in crisis that must change its pattern of ministry to reach its neighborhood. Our membership was made up with the largest group being women. The second largest group being non-working members, the elderly, and the retired. The age distribution further points up the situation at Southside. Between the ages of one to thirteen, we had eleven members, between the ages of thirteen to twenty we had thirty-eight, seven of which were regular attenders; between the ages of twenty-five to forty we had forty-two, eight of which were regular, forty-one years of age and up, we had 169 members, sixty of which were regular. From the distribution one can see the majority of Southside members were over forty-one years of age. The burden of ministry at Southside fell on those least able to give of themselves and their resources because of age. The age group needed for effective church leadership is twenty-five to forty. This potential leadership group was quite small and had few individuals who were committed and involved in the work of the church on a regular basis.

From an involvement standpoint 25 individuals held two or more positions in the church. Some of these served in as many as five different capacities. The leadership of Southside was vested in a small minority of the congregation. Involvement in church business was minimal. From October, 1974, through March, 1975, the average attendance at the regularly scheduled business meetings at Southside was ten. On different occasions the business meeting was held at the Sunday morning worship service in order to reach more people and have a quorum. A vast majority of the membership was unaware of the situation.

Sunday School—Sunday School enrollment had been on a decline, generally speaking, over the past ten years, ranging from a high enrollment of 466 in 1973 to a low of 325 in 1974. The average attendance for this ten year period had been up and down the scale. In 1973, the average monthly attendance in Sunday School was 121, with an average of 66 bus riders making up this figure. The children that were bused in were mostly black and made up 55 percent of the Sunday School, and on given Sundays this percentage was even higher.

The outreach of the Sunday School had been minimum. The outreach primarily had been in the children's division through the bus ministry. The adult division, which had five classes in 1973 and three classes in 1974, reached only five new members in two years. Some of these new members were serving as teachers in other divisions of the Sunday School. The Sunday School attendance stabilized to some degree, due largely to the dynamic and committed leadership of a new Sunday School director.

Church Training—Church Training as it is known throughout

the Southern Baptist Convention was no longer in existence as a structured entity at Southside Baptist Church in 1974. At one time Church Training had a high enrollment of 168. This occurred in 1970 and the enrollment in 1974 was 15. Thus Church Training was nonexistent for 1974-75.

Woman's Missionary Union—The WMU in the years 1964-74 had a high enrollment of 80 in 1967 and by 1973 was nonfunctional. What mission activity was carried on was due to the commitment of one woman to missions.

Brotherhood—The Brotherhood during the period 1964-74 had a high enrollment of 47 in 1966 and by 1970 was nonfunctional.

Baptisms and Other Additions—The evangelistic thrust of Southside Baptist Church remained constant. As seen in the Home Mission Board study, the evangelism thrust by churches in crisis communities is strong. However, this is only one side of the picture. While the thrust is strong, the new gain in resident members is low. Southside Baptist Church had a strong evangelistic thrust. Additions by letters were fewer than baptisms over the period 1969-74.

Financial Status—The per capita receipts for the period 1964-74 ranged from a low of 9.00 in 1964 to a high of 22.59 in 1974. This high per capita can be seen in the number of members supporting the church financially. In 1973, 74 members gave on some regular basis. While in 1974 that number decreased to 62. For the same period 1973-74 the number of members giving systematically decreased from 45 to 36. In 1974, 18 percent of Southside's total membership gave to the church on a regular basis, at the same time 12 percent of the resident membership gave to the church on a systematic basis.

The church appeared in the red eighteen different months in the years 1970-74. The budget of a little over three thousand a month was reached only once during 1974. Southside Baptist Church was constantly two to three hundred dollars below its

First Baptist Church today

needed weekly income. And this condition of deficit was constant over a four-year period.

Southside Baptist Church in 1975 had an indebtedness of seventy thousand dollars on its property. A piece of property that was referred to earlier (mission site) was leased out with an option to buy. The first six month agreement expired and was renewed by Southside Church. The option to buy was not picked up. Another lease agreement was entered into by the trustees of Southside Baptist Church on behalf of the church. That lease agreement ended and the option to buy was not exercised, and the lease agreement was not renewed. The offer made by the party leasing the property was not enough to pay off the indebtedness of Southside. Southside Baptist Church had therefore to assume an additional nine hundred dollars plus monthly payment on its indebtedness. It became unrealistic to assume that the membership could contribute an additional nine hundred dollars a month to take care of the mortgage payments, considering we were two to three hundred dollars below our budget each week as it was. Therefore, to assume that we could receive this additional sum each week was totally out of perspective. So Southside was forced into making some decision about its future, not only because of a ministry question but also because of a financial question.

Following an in-depth study of Southside over the past ten to eleven years, as pastor of the church I reached some conclusions concerning the future of our congregation.

1. Southside was a church in a crisis community. The first sign of this transition of the community occurred in 1963 and presented a problem to the church from that time to the present. The problem had advanced to such a stage that a search for possible solutions had to commence at once.

2. Due to loss in membership, decline in organizational structures, lack of financial resources, and lack of ability and resources to change its ministering patterns, Southside was too weak to be

an open congregation. Southside was losing ground with each passing year in its battle to remain functional in its mission to the community. Therefore Southside faced the necessity of making some decisive congregational decision about its future.

3. Unless some positive solutions were found, Southside would not exist in three to five years.

As the pastor of Southside Baptist Church I considered the options and alternatives that were mentioned earlier. Believing that God led me to Saint Petersburg and to Southside, I dedicated myself to the task of leading the church to the recognition of its problems and to working with the people in finding solutions. In 1975, Southside Baptist Church was standing at the crossroads of decision regarding its ministry and mission in the world.

SIX

Tabernacle Baptist Church

"The true and grand idea of a church is a society for the purpose of making men like Christ, earth like heaven, the kingdoms of the world the kingdom of Christ" (Thomas Arnold).

Originally, Tabernacle Baptist did not have a clear objective that was Christocentric because she was the product of strife. Like a great percentage of black congregations, a split gave birth to her. A split occurs when one congregation is plagued with differences which are never reconciled—at that point, the feuding congregation can no longer sing the hymn: We are not divided;/All one body we,/One in hope and doctrine,/One in charity.

In 1952, a pastor and a few members broke with the larger congregation and organized Tabernacle Baptist Church. I am convinced that much of the struggle encountered by Tabernacle in its first decade of existence can be directly attributed to the loose ends that brought about the split.

Are splits ever divine? I have searched for an answer—to no avail. I do think though that at times splits are justified!

In the case of Tabernacle Baptist, Satan meant it for evil but God, through many circumstances, turned it to good! The difficulties of those early days whittled a sizable congregation down to a faithful few—many of whom were not a part of the beginnings.

Two pastors preceded me and both of them made great attempts to lead the congregation into new areas of ministry locally, and denominationally. Tabernacle Baptist held membership in The South Florida Progressive Association, The Missionary and Educational Convention of Florida, and The National Baptist Convention of America.

In June, 1964, a new chapter began in my life and a turning point began in the life of Tabernacle. The memories are vivid and graphic . . . . A Sunday morning . . . church school was in session, a woman was presiding over about twenty-five people in attendance . . . seated on the podium was an old saged and seasoned eighty-year-old man; he was the pastor. I was a first time visitor. The woman superintendent shouted out with ecstasy, "Thank God, he has sent us help!" Little did I know that eighteen months later—sure enough, I would be installed as their third pastor. It happened January 24, 1966.

What has happened since then? Miracle upon miracle. This book is a testimony of just a few of the miracles.

What does a young man do when he has only been a Christian for two years, a minister for nine months and an eighty-year-old theologian who has preached for more than half a century says, "I am turning the teaching program over to you." At first I was filled with both delight and trepidation. Delight because of zeal and the opportunity, trepidation because of the responsibility thrust upon me being a novice in the faith. In addition, some of the people were not too pleasant—but I found insight from the words of Jeremiah 1:4–10: "The word of the Lord came unto me, saying, Before I formed thee in the belly I knew thee; and before thou camest forth out of the womb I sanctified thee, and I ordained thee a prophet unto the nations. Then said I, Ah, Lord God! behold, I cannot speak: for I am a child. But the Lord said unto me, Say not, I am a child: for thou shalt go to all that I shall send thee, and whatsoever I command thee thou shalt speak. Be not afraid of their faces: for I am with thee to deliver thee, saith the Lord. Then the Lord put forth his hand, and touched my mouth. And the Lord said unto me, Behold, I have put my words in thy mouth. See, I have this day set thee over the nations and over the kingdoms, to root out, and to pull down, and to destroy, and to throw down, to build, and to plant."

And so, on Wednesday evenings, the process of rooting out, pulling down, destroying, throwing down, building, and planting was instituted through a Bible teaching ministry. That went on for eighteen months before I became pastor. Little did we realize that those sessions were preparing us for a ministry of impact on a sizable segment of twentieth-century man.

Rooting Out

Traditionally, black congregations have suffered from an affliction I term a hiatus in leadership, mainly because of the economic status of trained ministers. The greater percentage of black congregations north, east, west, and south, fall into this category. Tabernacle was no exception. The word of God was used to root out the deep-seated paralysis of majoring in mediocrity. The rooting out process also dealt with the myth that says people with dark complexions are cursed, inferior, and must remain in a position of nonsignificance.

As the truth about God's word and his redemptive act through his son, Jesus Christ, began to penetrate and grip the hearts of God's people, many of them for the first time understood what Jesus meant when he said to a rabbi, "You must be born again." Many of the church members, including the chairman of the deacons, trusted Jesus Christ as personal Savior and began to follow him as Lord.

Following Jesus is the panacea for hang-ups. It matters not whether they are personal, cultural, or racial because Jesus paid it all. Rooting out was the most significant step in the process of forming an effective ministry.

Five Dimensions

The process of pulling down, destroying, throwing down, building, and planting is an ongoing undertaking. After eighteen months of teaching and moving among a people who were disfranchised in many ways, I received a call to take the helm of leadership.

Pulling Down

The letter of acceptance carried an attached proposed program of which all was accepted but one item. A spirit of expectancy swept throughout the congregation. Upward bound was the consensus of both the observers and those involved.

The pulling down process was one of rectification. A correct understanding of who God is and his ability "to do exceedingly abundantly above all we ask or think" is required because the possible is often frustrated when defeat is all one knows.

Destroying

There are times when rooting out and pulling down are not sufficient. Destruction is the surest and most productive measure. In our case, the Word of God destroyed superstitiousness, inferiority complexes, and the devastating mind-set that says we can't do this or that because of who we are.

The destruction of false notions and godless actions and attitudes set in motion a movement that has continued until this day. It is a movement of developing personal and interpersonal relationships. The movement has several supporting spokes: The ministry of personal evangelism, Christian stewardship, and family life ministries.

Throwing Down

In the process of time, the word got out into the community, and people from both the minority and the majority communities began to come and behold and participate in the evolution of a new kind of thrust in a despised community.

Paul's words about the Thessalonians reflect the early days of that ministry: "Our gospel came not unto you in word only, but

also in power, and in the Holy Ghost, and in much assurance; as
ye know what manner of men we were among you for your sake.
And ye became followers of us, and of the Lord, having received
the word in much affliction, with joy of the Holy Ghost: So that
ye were ensamples to all that believe in Macedonia and Achaia.
. . . also in every place your faith God-ward is spread abroad;
so that we need not to speak any thing. For they themselves shew
of us what manner of entering in we had unto you, and how ye
turned to God from idols to serve the living and true God"
(1 Thess. 1:5–9).

The throwing or spreading aspect was both prosperous and
painful. The pain came when others began to see a positive
change in the lives of the people and would often say, "You all are
different." It was most humiliating when it came from family and
fellow churchmen.

But the excitement of building and planting continued. Even
so, many of the people complained by frequently raising questions such as, why do we have to be so different from everybody
else? Why can't we do things like we used to? My own reply was,
what does the Word say?, or, it is not a matter of being like others
or doing what you used to do, instead, we need to have some
convictions and stand on them.

The Cultural Blend

The conviction to be biblical paid off in valuable and lasting
dividends. People from many walks of life came to worship
services and were relaxed in an atmosphere that was conducive
for blending cultures and establishing interracial relations and
friendships.

Surely, God was preparing us for a unique ministry. The Word
of God was proclaimed from Tabernacle's pulpit by white men,
Indians, Jamaicans, South Americans, and missionaries from
many countries of the world. The sincerity and sensitivity of the
people made deep impressions on the total community. Taberna-

cle grew in grace, in numbers, and in faithfulness to our God. In a word, at the age of twenty-two, Tabernacle Baptist was coming of age.

In 1973, the credentials committee of the Pinellas Baptist Association extended an invitation to the church for associational membership. In the annual session that same year, Tabernacle Baptist Church was graciously received with all the opportunities and privileges extended by an association. This congregational action was another milestone in the life of the church. God was up to something big! He had brought us a long way and we were continually learning what the church was, what she was to be and do.

"The church is never a place but always a people; never a fold, but always a flock, never a sacred building, but always a believing assembly.

"The church is you who pray, not where you pray.

"A structure of brick or marble can no more be a church than your clothes of serge or satin can be you.

"There is in this world nothing sacred but man, no sanctuary of God but the soul" (Anonymous).

A Testimony from a Young Couple

In 1971, I invited Jesus Christ into my life. For the next two months I had a lot of fellowship with a group of college students who, like me, were committed to Jesus Christ and wanted to change our communities, our country, and our world by confronting others with the claims of Jesus Christ. At the end of my sophomore year in college, I decided to transfer to a Christian school, therefore, I returned home. I came back to the church I was reared in with zeal and determination along with a vision to reach as many of my friends and other people in the city as possible. I also looked for other Christians to fellowship with, but to my surprise, I couldn't find any. It was during this time that I became confused, because I talked to many Christians who talked about the power of God and the Christian life, but I saw very little happening in their lives or in the many churches throughout the city. These people had little or no love for each other and no influence in the city.

Later that year, my new bride and I began looking for a church-home where Christ was in his place as head and where the Word was taught. At about this time, I started to investigate the life of one of my college teachers. I noticed that he was a man of vision and also a man of great moral character. The strange thing was that he seemed to really enjoy being a Christian. We began having fellowship regularly and I could see in him a burning desire to serve Jesus Christ, and I discovered that he was pastoring a church in my neighborhood.

Meanwhile, God had called me to preach while my wife and I were attending the church in which I grew up. I responded to the call and after a period of two months, I began to sense that God had a greater ministry in store for me. I transferred my membership to Tabernacle Baptist Church and my wife and I started a new life together in the church where my former college teacher pastored. We were very impressed with these people and their Christian life-styles. Not only did we sense the presence of God in their lives, they had a vision of fulfilling the Great Commission, but they also demonstrated a love for one another that could only be explained by the presence of God in the person of Jesus Christ. They welcomed us gladly into the fellowship, as well as their homes.

We were able to build new relationships and were challenged by the responsibilities that were given to us: working with the youth department, directing Sunday School, preaching, teaching and miscellaneous. For the next two years, we saw God work in a miraculous way at Tabernacle Baptist. That summer we took two bus loads of teens and adults to Explo '72 in Dallas, Texas. Our faith grew as God provided nearly $10,000 through Christian businessmen and friends in the community.

As the ministry continued to grow, the need arose for more full-time staff. Pastor Lampley recommended that I become his assistant. The whole church was excited about it because this was the first time we had had any full-time staff besides the pastor, and no other church in our community had an assistant pastor! The year of 1975 was a fruitful one indeed; our youth department grew, we had evangelism conferences for training Christians how to share their faith in Christ with others, we launched a bus ministry and a children's ministry and the Sunday School almost doubled in attendance. The black community was full of excitement about what God was doing through this church. I was ordained in May, 1975, and three other men of the fellowship were called of God to preach. Small groups of people began to meet together in homes for prayer. We felt that we were really experiencing revival. This was surely the ultimate of what God intended for us—a small group of people with the audacity to trust God. But God had just lead us another step in the direction that we were to go.—Richard and Janis Jackson, *former staff members of Campus Crusade for Christ International.*

Tabernacle's Influence on White Families

It had been one of those long, hot summers in Saint Petersburg during the late 1960's. The psychological line down Central Avenue was real and inflexible. It made a wide gulf between the north and the south parts of town. The dispute between the sanitation workers and the city fathers seemed insolvable. A garbage strike was imminent. The newspapers were playing it big! No one seemed to really care and the emissaries of peace— the city's churches, seemed particularly uninvolved. It was within this context that I talked with Mrs. Pat Schulert one day about the friendship and services she had shared with a group of black worshipers in south Saint Petersburg. I told her how distressed I felt over the churches' silence, how we had so often listened to tapes in our evening training sessions—voices from the white ghetto, the Mexican-Americans—and some token black welfare recipients. We seemed knowledgeable of the troubled areas, but unfamiliar with the troubled hearts. I told her too, how lucky she was to know and have black Christian friends. It was then that she asked if we too would like some black Christian friends.

The following Sunday evening after their church service, Pat entertained the Lewis Lampley family in her home and asked the Geyer family to join them. There was an immediate expression of warmth and love shared by all and we laughed over the chocolate and vanilla ice cream and our successful blend of black and white! Before long, Pastor Lampley made us aware of their present need for musicians in the church and wondered if we could fill in some Sunday for a morning service.

As we prepared for this first visit and hour of service—the only whites in a black church, we were encouraging one another that we were merely visiting; that we would try not to become too involved because of our own church responsibilities. Acquaintance turned to love and love turned us to paths of service in the family of Tabernacle Baptist Church.

There were moments during the years when we felt it was as unreal being the only whites in a black church as it was being in an all-white church, but we knew we were being loved by a people who, without question, would never find it necessary to march for their freedom. They had found it in Christ. They knew who they were and where they were going. They never held out a hand that said help me, rather they extended hearts full that cried let us help and love you.

We have received more than we have ever given, and we have delighted in sharing and watching the growth of the pastor loving and leading his flock. The greatest joy is witnessing the response of the people to the message of God's love—to be aware of the renewed and vital love and compassion in the hearts of the people.

First Baptist before remodeling

May it come to pass that more and more faces of the flock are not identified by color, and the line down Central Avenue will disappear (Betty and Allen Geyer, Saint Petersburg, Florida, January, 1977).

Harold Brigham's verse on Life is fitting:

Empty chairs and vacant places
Soon will fill with other faces;
New will come where old have gone,
Eternal change goes on and on.

At this point, it is necessary for me to digress and bring to your attention some events that clearly point to the fact that God was at work simultaneously in both the black congregation (Tabernacle Baptist) and in the white congregation (Southside Baptist). History shows that Southside Baptist Church had flourished for some twenty-six years, but now it was on the wane. Let's hear the story from one of the deacons. His story begins with the year, 1966.

A Deacon's View

If anyone had thought that Southside was going to dry up, they soon found out differently. Sam Jordan, Jr., was the biggest man I have ever seen. (In God's work, that is.) Many outstanding programs were begun under Sam's ministry. The church started having a Wednesday evening meal and visitation program that reached many people. Members who had never been involved in such a program were surprised at what they could do with some training and the Holy Spirit's help—with the community being more mixed racially by now, it was not uncommon to visit an address and be welcomed by a black man or lady.

Brother James Bedwell, a man in his eighties and a member of Southside for more than a dozen years, showed us all how to be an unprejudiced Christian. Brother Bedwell was an ordained preacher, having studied at Mercer. He was from Tennessee, but no man from the north or south ever loved God or his fellowman anymore than he did. He walked the neighborhood and passed out tracts and other materials. I remember well the deacon's meeting when Brother Bedwell asked what he should do if a black person expressed a desire to attend Southside. No one spoke for a minute, then Sam Jordan said, "Invite them. I have no qualms or mixed feelings about ministering to black people or any other race."

Looking back now, one can see how God had a plan for Southside. He sent Rev. Carlos Owens to speak to us and help us to participate in the 1969 Crusade of America Revival. Brother Owens and his wife were missionaries to Tanzania, Africa. It was the most exciting revival we ever held.

Southside took on a special project to help a native church, in a village called Msekela, to rebuild a church building that had been destroyed. Nearly $1,000 was raised for this work. Southside had nearly every year given about $1,000 to the Lottie Moon Offering. But we all seemed to have a very special desire to help in this cause. Brother Owens has been back again, and there is certainly a warm tie between Southside and him.

Churches were getting involved in bus ministries everywhere—so Sam began working on the folks who would be logical workers. Lillian Anderson and my wife, Mattie, went with Sam to a bus clinic in Orlando, Florida. It was sponsored by Ray Sadler and his team. A sad note here—Ray Sadler was to hold a bus clinic at Southside but along with two members of his team, was killed in a plane crash just a few days before the clinic date. We were not to be denied such a blessing though, so we purchased an old Ford bus, and the young people really fixed it up. Ginger Anderson and Sherrill Hill made it the happiest looking bus on the streets. Lillian was our first bus captain, and then we got another bus, and Mattie answered her calling. No two women ever worked harder on any project than those two bus captains. Brother Bill Boro, a retired Air Force captain and super pilot and mechanic, put in many hours in our bus ministry. At this time, Brother Harry Walker, also a driver, as was Brother Boro, spent many hours with the buses.

It was about this time that a black youth named Michael Ammons began riding one of the buses. We had fifty or sixty black children riding our buses and maybe about twelve adults attending Sunday School and church. Some had been accepted into the membership by letter. Michael made a profession of faith in Jesus and was baptized into the church, thus becoming the first black person to be baptized into a Pinellas County Association, Florida Baptist Southern Baptist Convention affiliated church.

A young man dropped into Sam's office one day asking if we needed a pianist. This is how one of the most talented and lovable persons that you could ever meet came to us. Of course, I'm referring to Les Lommich. Besides playing the piano, organ, and bagpipes (wearing kilts and all), he brought many a tear to our eyes with his wonderful voice. He was a wizard with electronics and tape recordings. Quite often he would accompany himself (via tape) while singing. "The King Is Coming" was simply outstanding. His wife, Linda, and daughter, Leslie, were always in the services and helped make up a wonderful church with a sweet, sweet spirit. At Sam's request, we adopted "Sweet, Sweet Spirit" as our church's inspirational theme.

With the buses doing such a good job, we were having quite a number of children ages five to eleven in the worship service. With this energy being released it became a matter to deal with.

At the beginning of service one Sunday morning, I was in the pulpit giving the Sunday School report. When I finished, I announced to the children that we were going to begin having children's church right then and to follow me. With the two Jordan girls, Laura and Linda, and a fifteen-year-old black youth, Alphonso Miller helping, children's church was begun with nearly fifty children.

So was the ministry of one "Uncle Bill," and I have enjoyed every minute of this work. I would recommend to any church that does not have a youth church, to start one. Wonderful books are available and if your church personnel can attend a clinic put on by Gardner Gentry, it will be most rewarding. To this day, our youth church has up to 110 in attendance.

Age was taking its toll and we lost several saints of the church. If churches had a hall of fame, members such as Mrs. T. T. Cox, Miss Lou Ina Bates, Uncle John Cheshire, James Bedwell, Uncle Bill Hardin, and Jerry Schroeder would certainly be in it.

Sam had begun work on his doctorate and while on vacation, became known to a church in Kentucky. Eventually, he accepted a call to the Elkhorn Baptist Church in Lexington, Kentucky. He closed his ministry at Southside on June 15, 1974. It can truly be said of Dr. Sam Jordan, Jr. that he practiced what he preached about being brothers in Christ.

A pulpit committee was elected, and the search for a pastor was begun. With the church in a terrible financial strain, the membership began to show the effects of the pressure. Special prayer was held on special occasions and you could actually feel the presence of the Holy Spirit. Bill Guess, our association missionary, was meeting with us, praying with us, and along with his assistant shared our burdens. And once again, God showed that he has the man for the job.

After contacting and making the necessary arrangements, Rev. Delos Sharpton came to Saint Petersburg and preached at the Friendship Baptist Church. The pulpit committee was very impressed. Delos was well qualified. He attended Samford College at Birmingham and also was a Southern Seminary graduate. He was involved in programs that were integrated and pastored a church in Indiana. He was born and raised in Gadsden, Alabama, but certainly was free from any prejudice. No young preacher ever began such an unusual ministry, for it seemed that the beginning was the start of the work that would be the end.

Though we were at this time well integrated, and with a fairly good attendance, we had to face reality. Survival in the present economy was impossible. We began to explore ways and means of continuing. Reorganizing was discussed, but did not seem to be the answer. A retreat was scheduled for the church leadership to meet at Moon Lake (our Pinellas Association assembly grounds) with Bill Guess and Ray Dobbin of Jacksonville.

After many prayers and discussions, Bill Guess began to reveal a plan for merging Southside with Tabernacle Baptist. Tabernacle, under the leadership of Rev. Lewis C. Lampley, had grown until they were cramped for space. Also they, along with Mt. Carmel Baptist of Clearwater, had become affiliated with the Southern Baptist Convention.

The recommendation was well received by the group and was proposed to the church. The church voted to merge. September 7, 1975, was the date set to merge. The settling of debts and transferring of properties was done. Our pastor went with the First Baptist Church and Rev. Lampley was to pastor the church now incorporated as "Southside Tabernacle Baptist Church."

We have completed a year now and some of the former members moved their memberships. Among the newly received members, many are Caucasian.

A church that seemed destined to disintegrate, instead became integrated and is probably the busiest church in Saint Petersburg. We who are a minority are enjoying the greatest experience of our Christian lives.

Mark Wolfe, our Southside choir director, continued on and as a result, we have a very good musical program.

I was elected chairman of the deacon committee and it has been a real blessing to my life as we worship together. This unique black-white congregation can be described with one word: "Wonderful!" (William G. Bryan, Sr., Chairman, Deacon Committee, Southside Tabernacle Baptist Church Saint Petersburg, Florida).

SEVEN

An Impulse of the Spirit

In the spring of 1975, Delos Sharpton, the young pastor of Southside Baptist Church, called one day and invited me to go to lunch with him and the director of missions of Pinellas Baptist Association, Bill Guess. The invitation was accepted with no thought of what was about to transpire. During the lunch, the young pastor related his call to serve the Southside Baptist Church and his consequent problems. He indicated that when he had discussed coming to the church with the pulpit committee, they had talked of the fact that the community was in transition and the shape of the ministry would be determined by the changes occurring within the community.

He had accepted the call to the church, so he told us, with the understanding that the church understood its community and was willing and ready to minister to the needs of the people surrounding their church. However, in the period of time that he had been there, he had discovered that the people of the church did not really grasp the implications of the fact that the community had gradually shifted from white to black in percentage of residents. Furthermore, the church was experiencing serious decline in membership, financial resources, and was losing its attractiveness to new residents in surrounding neighborhoods, as well as their own. He rather graphically outlined to the two of us the kinds of problems that they were having.

Since Delos had not given me any information prior to that luncheon concerning his problem, when he asked me for a suggestion, there was certainly no way that a well-thought plan could be set forth. Yet, very easily an idea came to mind that was suggested. It had to do with a three-way merger between Southside Baptist Church, her nearest neighbor, Tabernacle Baptist Church, and the church I served, First Baptist Church. At that time, I would have had no difficulty in assessing the idea as being an impulse of the Spirit. Certainly in the months that followed that meeting, there was absolutely no question that the merger was an idea of the Holy Spirit.

As is so often true, that which was an impulse of the Spirit at the time to us, had been in formation for some time. A number of factors came into proper perspective that day. Of no little consequence in preparation for that meeting were the first responsibilities I had been asked to take in the association upon my coming to serve First Baptist. I was asked to serve as the chairman of the credentials committee. Though that assignment is not usually an imposing office or task, I was aware upon agreement to serve that I had been asked because circumstances were not routine at that time. A black Baptist church had petitioned for fellowship in our association and at least two others were considering similar action. Such a matter, even in 1972, required careful leadership and the commitment of the larger churches in the association.

Only one of the churches followed through with the petition for fellowship in Pinellas Association that year. The church request was routinely presented and received with warmth and enthusiasm, with no negative feelings manifested in any way. The very fine pastor of that congregation and a number of the members of the Mt. Carmel Baptist Church of Clearwater were welcomed as brothers in Christ to cooperate in the mission endeavor of Baptists through the Pinellas Association.

The acceptance of the Mt. Carmel Baptist Church was of signal importance from many standpoints. It marked their willingness to trust us after years of frustration and broken fellowship. It offered to white Baptists in Pinellas County an opportunity to grow in grace and express an appropriate Christian love in accepting these brothers in Christ as just that—brothers in Christ. Not only was the opportunity present to take a step that was honorable, just, and right, but also the opportunity was present to take a step that could become catalytic to other advances in the months ahead.

The action that year in the association served to break some of the barriers in the minds and hearts of people concerning the working together of blacks and whites in God's service. Even at that time the Southside Baptist Church had a few black people attending the services without any problem and other churches in the Association had some black children attending Sunday School through the bus ministry. First Baptist Church had several black children who had been enlisted through the bus ministry and who, on occasion, attended church. Several young women in the church were active in a ministry called Project Playpen, which was an effort in cooperation with other churches and social agencies to train black mothers to operate day care centers in their homes. There were other indications of a growing attitude of Christian concern and love toward our black brethren, but all of us were a long way from accomplishing a real breakdown of the walls of separation.

The factors before mentioned concerning the predominance of older white adults in the downtown section of the city has a bearing upon the attitude of First Baptist Church in respect to racial understanding, also. Most churches who face all of the problems of being downtown, certainly have faced the reality of blacks and other ethnic groups moving into the vacated retail and housing buildings in the vicinity of the church. Not only racial overtones but economic problems must be met and faced realistically in that instance. However, the problem surrounding First Baptist had never been black ghetto, but increasing numbers of older white adults with limited income. This factor caused First Baptist to face a different problem from that of many downtown churches. Consequently, there had not been the kind of confrontation with racial discrimination and maturation in expressing Christian grace that many other downtown churches had faced. Of course, that also means that First Baptist had not faced the kinds of situations that can harden attitudes in the negative vein either.

Thus, the acceptance of Mt. Carmel Baptist Church into the fellowship of Pinellas Baptist Association offered the opportunity to First Baptist Church, along with others, to experience the Christian character of black Baptists and debunk some of the myths and assumptions called prejudice. It was not an instantaneous process of perfection, but it offered the kind of real life experience that serves to eliminate fears and misconceptions. In no small way it was a beginning of that impulse of the Spirit that was consummated several years later.

Equally important to the opportunity for white Baptists to experience fellowship with their black brothers in Christ and thus develop better understanding, was the opportunity for the black Baptists to learn that not all white Baptists felt enmity and discrimination toward the black people. There is little doubt that the good experience of the Mt. Carmel Baptist Church in joining the fellowship of the Pinellas Baptist Association and the Florida Baptist State Convention, served to prepare the way for the later addition of the Tabernacle Baptist Church to the Pinellas Baptist Association. When word spread of the eager and enthusiastic participation of the members of Mt. Carmel Baptist Church and their warm welcome by the fellowship of Pinellas Baptist Association, in due time Tabernacle Baptist Church likewise petitioned for fellowship in the association and was received just as warmly.

What seemed to us that day at lunch as an impulse had been in the developmental stage in the purpose of the Spirit for some time. Had not the Tabernacle Baptist Church been in cooperative fellowship with the Pinellas Association at the time the merger was first conceived, there would have been little likelihood of the suggestion being offered, let alone entertained seriously.

Moreover, had not the people of Tabernacle felt Christian fellowship and acceptance with the Baptists of Pinellas County, there would have been no need to approach them with such a suggestion. A very vital ingredient for success had been in the process long before the three of us met for lunch that spring day. It was without a doubt, an impulse of the Spirit.

Several realities pressed our sensitivities that day at the lunch table. A three-way merger might be possible, but there were many problems. Three churches would need to be led to understand the motivations and implications of the suggestion. First, Southside would have to face so many emotions concerning a drastic shift in ministry and an apparent giving away of their facilities to a black congregation. The black congregation would naturally face the doubts and distrust of such a preposterous idea as someone giving them a building. First Baptist would have to face all of these same thoughts plus the question, "Why should we be involved since it is not our problem?"

Two very obvious problems came to the surface that first day. One had to do with a serious financial problem of the Southside Baptist Church. Due to some improvements to their property and the purchase of some property for a mission site, the church had an indebtedness of approximately seventy thousand dollars. The black congregation, indeed any congregation, would have an understandable suspicion of anyone who came seeking to give them something including a seventy thousand dollar debt. It was the consensus that if the debt were not removed from the proposal there would not be much opportunity for serious conversation concerning the merger. Thus, the idea for a third partner in the merger was conceived, with First Baptist Church assuming the indebtedness. In the light of all the factors discussed previously, an additional seventy thousand dollars seemed formidable at that time.

There crossed my mind that day the thought that if somehow our church could take the challenge to assume that debt and thus help facilitate the merger, it very well could forestall a dream I shared with some for First Baptist Church to purchase the hotel adjacent to our property. Still it seemed the most visible and viable possibility. So a basic element of the proposal would be for First Baptist to be challenged to accept the responsibility for discharging the debt. It was agreed that there was no need for that to be considered until Southside and Tabernacle were agreed to the basic idea of a merger involving the membership of Tabernacle moving into the facilities of Southside church.

A second fundamental problem occurred that day in the first discussions. It was not too pleasant to admit, but we all knew that it was a reality that must be considered, it had to do with the future of Delos Sharpton. It was quite obvious that the merged church did not need two preachers. Though they could use additional staff, their need did not include both Delos Sharpton and Lewis Lampley. Though no discussions had taken place with Lewis Lampley at that time, it was quickly agreed that he was the logical one to be the pastor of the new fellowship if it came into being. He was well equipped for the ministry and was most capable of ministering to the blacks and whites in the merged fellowship. It was assumed that the predominance of black membership would be better served by the black minister. In no way did we desire to cause or even allow a contest to develop around the two ministers that could issue in any kind of hurt to either man or the church. Thus, it was determined that if any merger occurred, some alternative should be developed for Delos.

In considering an alternative for Delos Sharpton several factors were obvious. As a young man he had faced a very trying situation which was likely to become more taxing and disillusioning. That assumption proved to be very true. It was felt that Delos needed a nurturing fellowship in which he could be encouraged and in which he could receive further development as a minister. Another realistic matter involved the possibility of his making a move to another fellowship. Though it was not the most pleasant

Southside Tabernacle Baptist, formerly Southside

prospect, it was obviously true that Delos would have a difficult time being called to a church from a racially mixed church, certainly one in which the predominance of members were black. Time proved that assumption to be true, for several churches would politely but quickly dismiss consideration of this very fine young minister when they learned that he had led his church to participate in a merger with a black congregation. That which was immensely to his credit was to become a burden in the eyes of some. Thus, the only possible approach to solving the dilemma concerning the future of Delos Sharpton seemed to be for him to become an assistant pastor at First Baptist Church. That idea became another vital ingredient in the plan that first day.

The prospect of taking the indebtedness of Southside Baptist Church posed some serious problems in my mind insofar as the challenge it offered First Baptist. Now, to add to that responsibility the proposition of adding a staff member we could not afford was a serious concern. As already mentioned, in order to deal with financial problems in First Baptist Church, reorganization of the staff had been effected in which some assignments were combined and a staff position eliminated. That reorganization was made possible when a young assistant pastor had been called to his own charge. The experience of the church in years past with young men who had recently graduated from the seminary had been very positive; so the idea of a young assistant, in itself, would not be rejected.

The proposition from the beginning took the shape that it sustained through the consummation of the merger. One, First Baptist Church would assume the seventy thousand dollar debt of the Southside Baptist Church to facilitate the discussions. Two, Delos Sharpton would be transferred to the staff of First Baptist Church to be an assistant pastor until the Lord was ready to move him to another place of responsibility.

The anticipated obstacles to the successful participation of First Baptist Church were at least threefold. First, there would be some who would question the motivation and implications of our involvement with a black church. Because of the suspicions built up over the years on the part of both black and white individuals, it is often difficult to accept the fact that there is simply no ulterior design on the part of anyone in such a venture as the proposed merger. Another aspect to the racial implications was that the Southside Baptist Church was integrated and it was entirely possible that in the merger some of the black members of Southside might prefer to come to First Baptist Church rather than stay in the merged fellowship of Southside and Tabernacle.

Second, there would be the very real and understandable apprehension concerning the acceptance of further financial obligation in the light of the commitments First Baptist already had.

Third, there would be the concern that our attention, energies, and resources ought to be concentrated on our own needs in the downtown church with all the problems that we had facing us for the future. That is a concern always present in some form in any church that seeks to be involved in missions beyond itself.

The meeting that day for lunch seemed to be of relatively minor import at the time. Delos apparently had derived some hope from the interchange of ideas and was obviously stimulated to tackle a very difficult challenge. His task, both in convincing his own church and in approaching the black congregation and engaging dialogue, seemed so formidable that I suppose I really did not face the full impact of what I had agreed to challenge First Baptist Church to do. Yet, I felt very good about the prospects of what seemed a very exciting proposition that could answer the needs of two churches and stimulate a third.

One of the most lasting effects of the merger to my own personal life is the increasing conviction that the Holy Spirit led us that day in laying the groundwork for an action that he had been preparing to accomplish for some time. It is always exciting to be a part of whatever God happens to be doing in the community in which you live. After all, that is what ministry is all about.

EIGHT

An Idea Is Born

The transition of a community from one race to another, from one economic level to another, and from one social level to another is today's facts. Churches have moved, closed their doors, sold their property, and ended their ministry because their familiar neighborhoods have changed. The churches in transitional neighborhoods and communities often reach the point where they realize they can no longer make a viable contribution to their community because of the radical change that has occurred. Churches like Southside have gone from being an aggressive church reaching out to its community, to a church just struggling for survival. The experiences and emotions of the people surface in clear and understandable human terms, as the situation at Southside gave evidence. I recall some of our people saying: "What do I do now? I helped build the church; I gave all that I had and now I am watching it disappear before my eyes. What do I do now? This is the only church I have ever belonged to. I raised my family in this church and community, now I feel isolated and cut off from what I love the most."

It is difficult for churches to acknowledge that they are in a crisis community and to face some difficult decisions. Personally, I think a church should not wait until its community changes to evaluate its existence and its mission. This should be an ongoing project. The church should always be seeking how it can reflect Christ in its community and the world. However, human nature being what it is, a time of crisis is the catalyst that moves us to reflection and action. The crisis of a changing neighborhood caused Southside Church to begin the process of reflecting and wrestling with that great question: What is the church and what can we do to insure the continuing ministry of our church?

This was a new situation for me personally. Having entered the ministry at age fifteen, many experiences had been mine, but not anything to help me deal with a community in transition. I recall during the early days of 1975, reflecting back on my call to the ministry and my early concepts of the ministry and the church. As a fifteen-year-old I conceived the ministry as being like the ministry of Billy Graham. You travel, preach, share your faith and everyone tells you what a good preacher you are. The years have a way of weeding out those naive thoughts and patterns of the ministry. Through experience, college, and seminary, one develops beyond these early concepts and ideas. This is that sense of becoming that the Christian pilgrimage is all about. At Southside a whole new world was to open before my eyes. For the first time in fourteen years, the true ministry of the church and what it is all about began to come in focus. For like the church, the transitional community had called me to reflect and think deeply on our mission in the world as individual ministers, people, and as a corporate body. The days and months that followed were to become some of the most difficult of my ministry but some of the most challenging.

Where does one begin in trying to explain a personal and corporative pilgrimage? Perhaps the place to begin is with the role of the pastor. The pastor of a church sets the direction and pace for the congregation. He creates the atmosphere that permeates the church. If he is loving, his people respond in like fashion. If he moves in a progressive manner, more likely than not the church will follow. Realizing one's position and coming to grips with it is all important. Any pastor, but especially a pastor of a church located in a transitional community, must know who he is and allow the Father to lead him. Therefore, once I faced the situation of pastoring a church in a transitional community and made my decision to stay, one battle had been won. Commitment is necessary to have a productive ministry; within the context of a transitional community, it is an all-important factor.

With a deep commitment to be the kind of pastor Southside Church needed, I began the process of setting the pace, direction, and tone of the ministry of the church as I understood it. However, in the end the people of God in the individual church decide the church's future. The pastor of a church in a transitional neighborhood must give leadership to his people, as they struggle with a very present reality. Both pastor and people must thoughtfully and prayerfully seek God's will to be done regardless of personal feelings or desires. What follows is an account of a journey taken by one pastor and church.

When a pastor moves onto a new church field, one of the first things he faces is establishing trust with his people. This is true for a pastor who comes to serve a church in a transitional community as well. Once I had discovered and realized that Southside Baptist Church was in a transitional community and made a commitment to stay and look for a solution, I immediately encountered this element of trust. In the final analysis, a pastor can do no more than his people allow him to do. A pastor always hopes that his people will trust him, respect him, and believe in his ministry. This is even more important as a pastor of a transitional church begins his ministry.

Having been at Southside less than a year, I was very much aware of the need to establish a relationship of trust and respect with my people. I did not know what the future held in relationship to Southside Church and the situation it faced. I did not know what kind of decisive action would have to be taken and how the people would react to it. I soon found however, that I did not have to worry about the membership of Southside Church trusting me, respecting me, and accepting my leadership. Quite the contrary, they were very open and receptive to me and to my ministry. Usually a pastor feels like it will take anywhere from a year to two years to build up the kind of relationship with his people to carry out the ministry that is needed. This had been my thinking up to this point and juncture of my ministry. However, I soon learned that the people of Southside were ready to be led in a strong and decisive manner.

Although they found it hard to understand all that had happened in regard to the changing community, it was clear to the most apathetic member that things were not as they should be. In retrospect, I believe the situation aided in the establishing of trust, mutual respect, and acceptance. As I look back now, it was remarkable that this church, that had been declining for several years, could welcome a young man and his family right out of seminary and open their hearts as they did. I believe the love that these people had to give was the greatest single contributing factor to the success in what was to follow.

With a strong feeling that I was loved, accepted, and trusted as the pastor of Southside Baptist Church, I felt comfortable in moving toward exerting strong leadership in seeking solutions to the existing situation. One of the first things that I felt needed to be done, was to stabilize the present membership. Since 1963 and the first encounter with blacks in their community, the people of Southside had begun to despair. It was up to me to rekindle a feeling of hope, after all this should be one of the major tasks of any pastor.

For the Christian church to minister effectively, its people must have hope in the Father, in one another, and in the ministry and mission of the church. Several things were undertaken to help create an atmosphere of hope. Churchwide fellowships were held to bring the people together in a oneness of spirit. Worship services were geared to create an atmosphere of family and concern for one another. A pastoral visitation program was established so that the people could know that their pastor cared about them as individuals.

The organizations of the church needed to become stable.

Sunday School teachers and workers needed encouragement, on several occasions many teachers came to Sunday School and found no one to teach. Appreciation luncheons were held for those who had made vital contributions to Southside Baptist Church. Cleanup days were held in an effort to help the people regain pride in their church. The physical plant at Southside had undergone several years of deterioration. Work days were held to make necessary repairs in order to keep the church functional and attractive. The effort to improve the attractiveness of the physical plant also gave the people some concrete activity to be involved in. These things strengthened the sense of fellowship, the sense of belonging, and the sense of a community of believers.

Before the congregation could make any concrete decision about the future, the present had to be secure. Therefore as pastor it became necessary for me to establish some priorities in relationship to the work of our church. Before our people could handle the future they had to be able to have hope in the present. For the first six months of my ministry at Southside I gave myself to securing the present, hoping we could then secure the future.

In my interviews with the pastoral selection committee, one of the concerns they expressed to me was the financial condition of Southside Church. Before I accepted the pastorate they were very honest, open, and frank with me concerning the finances. During our discussions, the ray of hope they expressed for the church financially was the selling of the mission property, which had been purchased for a mission site in 1966. It was their belief that if the asking price of one hundred thousand dollars was met, Southside Church could pay off its indebtedness, and have a surplus to use as resource funding for ministry to the church and to the community. In our discussions they further shared with me that the property was presently leased to an Independent Baptist Church with a clause which gave this group an option to buy the property. They expressed to me the desire of the Independent Baptist Church to purchase the property at the asking price, thereby aiding Southside Baptist Church and giving it a much stronger financial base.

Upon becoming pastor of Southside Baptist Church, I understood more fully the committee's concern with regard to Southside's financial base. I learned that the number of people contributing on a regular basis had declined over the last four years. I also learned that the average monthly offering had declined over the last several years. The church was also fifteen hundred to two thousand dollars below their budget requirements monthly. I felt like it was imperative to do a study not only of the financial situation of Southside but also of the entire church over a ten-year period beginning in 1964 and running through the year ending 1974. This study would be most helpful in setting the stage for some definite congregational action with regard to the future of Southside Baptist Church.

By January 1975, it became apparent to me that an effort had to be made to find some solutions, especially to the critical financial situation. The church could not continue to run with a deficit bank balance every month. At the January deacon's meeting, the deacons and I discussed the present situation as it affected our community, ministry, and finances. It was resolved that attention must be given to the future.

I met the next day with the attorney that represented Southside Church. We discussed the legal aspects of the lease agreement with the Independent Baptist Church and the possible recourse if the lease were broken and if they did not exercise the option to purchase the property. I felt like it was imperative that I understood the legal ramifications of our lease agreement with the Independent Baptist Church, our obligations to the three lending institutions which held mortgages on our property and what arrangements could be made with these institutions if this option to purchase the mission property was not exercised.

After meeting with our attorney, I met with the pastor of the

Independent Baptist Church which was presently leasing the mission property. I shared the situation as we saw it at Southside with regard to our needs, hopes, and desires for our continuing ministry in our present location. I shared with him my concern regarding their desires to purchase the property. He reassured me that his church was very much interested in the property, thought the asking price was fair, would do everything within their power at the end of the lease period to exercise their option. Soon after my meeting with the pastor of the Independent Baptist Church, I met with the president of one of the local banks concerning the financial situation at Southside Church. The president of the bank was a member of Southside Church and had served as treasurer and been a big asset in administering the financial resources of Southside Church. The bank held several notes, and therefore, I wanted to discuss with him our intent to pay off those notes at the close of the agreement with the Independent Baptist Church. A word must be said about this man and his efforts. It is my opinion that without the efforts of this man the situation at Southside would have been critical many years prior to my coming as pastor. This man served in a most admirable fashion. He served the church as financial counselor and was in a position to assist the church in any way possible through his office. It was and is my conviction that a church must be responsible in the financial area of its ministry. So I tried to administer the budget in such a way that we were always able to meet our financial obligations. At this juncture all we could do as a church was wait for the lease agreement period to end and trust that the option to buy would be exercised.

At the same time we were trying to administer our ministry resources in the best way possible. It became imperative that we let our church and community know that we were still there to minister. In January 1975, I attended a planning meeting of Southside area churches to consider a medical-dental unit owned by the Florida Baptist Convention to be used in the community.

I felt like this was an honest effort to get the feel of the community and also afford us an opportunity to let it be known to our community that we wanted to minister.

The medical-dental unit came to Southside Baptist Church during the month of February 1975, and local dentists, dental hygienists, and their assistants ministered in a very physical way to the people of our church and our community. To me this was a very outward expression of concern and of ministry. It was encouraging to me to see several of the members of Southside Church working with these people, helping to interpret what dental work would be done, and sharing with them the gospel of the Lord Jesus Christ.

In this same vein I contacted an organization called Operation Neighborhood Alert. Operating through the Saint Petersburg Police Department, a representative came to our church on a Wednesday evening and presented to our congregation the need of preventing crime in the community. I believed that this would make our congregation aware of the need of preventing crime and at the same time would show them the need for community cooperation. One of the main ingredients of this crime prevention program was a neighbor assisting a neighbor approach. In a transitional community, this is one of the greatest needs, for neighbors to trust one another.

In February of 1975, we held an Adult Valentine Banquet designed to foster fellowship and unity among the adults of our church. Opportunities for the church to share together helped create and sustain a sense of hope and fostered a deeper love for one another. During this same period our Sunday School attendance and our worship service attendance stabilized. There appeared to be some relief from the tension that had built up during the absence of a pastor and the lack of a structured effort to continue the mission of the church.

The same month, I met with the director of missions for the Pinellas Baptist Association and discussed at length with him the present situation and the future of Southside Baptist Church. Upon his recommendation I conferred on several occasions with his assistant who was the Christian social minister of the Pinellas Baptist Association. We explored together possible community ministries and ways that our people could be involved in reaching out to the community. The mobile medical unit had been a very positive event for Southside Church. This made other community ministries feasible. One of the community ministry services that we discussed centered in letting the community know that Southside Church was still functioning. In March, two local precincts were located at the church so that the people of the community could vote in the city elections. This again was an effort to create community involvement within our church and to establish our identification in the community.

By mid-March I had concluded the ten-year study of Southside Baptist Church and sought to evaluate my findings. After examining this study and seeing exactly where we were statistically over the ten-year period 1964-1974, it became increasingly clear to me that to secure the future ministry of Southside Baptist Church, efforts had to begin immediately to find solutions to the problems we were facing. I became convinced that many of the members of Southside Church did not understand exactly what had taken place over the last ten years. In an effort to inform and to make the membership aware of what was happening in our church, the monthly business meeting was moved from a Wednesday evening to the Sunday morning worship service. This was done because many times we would have only six or seven members present on Wednesday evening to conduct the business of the church. By moving the business meeting I hoped more concern and involvement would be created.

Following my evaluation of the study numbering some thirty pages including charts and graphs, I contacted the director of the Pinellas Baptist Association to brief him on my findings and let him evaluate the study. In our meeting we discussed Southside's

Former Tabernacle Baptist

situation: past, present, and future. It was his belief that the state of the church did need immediate attention. In an effort to seek as much outside assistance as possible, I contacted the director of the Cooperative Missions Department of the Florida Baptist Convention to come to Saint Petersburg and discuss the situation we faced as a church. I did so realizing that although I was relatively new to the situation at Southside, I still was pastor of the church. I realized that pastors have a bad record of trying to lead a church in such a situation. But it was my conviction that sometimes an outside person is needed to pull data together and help the people on their own to come face to face with the very real situation.

The director of Corporate Missions for Florida State Convention graciously consented to come and meet with me. The director of missions for Pinellas Baptist Missions, the director of Cooperative Missions, and I reviewed my findings and discussed possible solutions. The study that I had compiled clearly revealed a church in a crisis community.

I wanted to use every outside resource that I possibly could, so I also contacted Dr. Jim Graves, pastor of First Baptist Church, Saint Petersburg, who then was serving as president of the Florida Baptist Convention. This was an effort on my part to seek further counseling and guidance with regard to the Southside situation. One of the grave dangers that I saw still hanging over me was the possibility that I would reach the point that I felt like I could do it all myself or that I would become so discouraged and leave the situation altogether. It became imperative to me therefore, if I intended to seek God's will for the church to which he had called me that I not refuse the help and assistance of anyone. So along with the director of the Pinellas Association, Dr. Graves met with us in March of 1975, for a briefing on the Southside situation. (One thing must be added that meant so much during this time of searching and seeking possible solutions. The fact that members of the state convention staff, those from the Pinellas Baptist Association, or Dr. Graves never attempted to bully or bypass me in order to find a solution. These people showed a willingness and a readiness to help.)

During that luncheon meeting with Dr. Graves we discussed the Southside situation, the contents of my study, and the feelings that I had as to possible solutions. I shared with Dr. Graves at this time some of the discussions that I had with others of the state convention, association, and others. We discussed with Dr. Graves one alternative that the rest of us had examined and discussed: the possibility of merging Southside Church with another Southern Baptist church in the city that was in the midst of a struggling situation itself. At first, we looked at this as a viable alternative from having to close the church or have a foreclosure. The idea being, that perhaps two struggling churches could secure a future together. However, we went on to share with him that really we did not see this as a viable alternative, because we did not feel like there was another white congregation that could be merged.

Following a brief discussion of the situation, Dr. Graves made a very interesting and at that time a very improbable proposal. He suggested that perhaps a merger with a predominantly black church might secure the ministry in a community which was predominantly black. He went on to state that perhaps a three-way merger could occur, whereby the presently constituted Southside Baptist Church could merge with a predominantly black congregation and a larger, more established church would assume the indebtedness of Southside Church so that the newly merged church could be strong. Our thoughts at that meeting began to turn to possible churches. After giving some thought to this, the name of Tabernacle Baptist Church came up. A predominantly black church and a member of the Pinellas Baptist Association and the Southern Baptist Convention, it was growing and expanding beyond its present facilities. We knew that the Tabernacle Baptist Church was one of the fastest growing churches in our area. This suggestion of a rather unusual merger of three churches was heard with a degree of wonder, of possibility, and of fear. We left that luncheon meeting resolved to commit this discussion to prayer and thoughtful consideration.

As the pastor of Southside Baptist Church, I heard the idea as a strong possible solution for crisis. However, I could not fathom in my wildest dreams and imagination how it could occur. I wondered what would happen within the Southside Church if such a thing was proposed. In a very personal vein, I wondered what would happen to me. Regardless of how far we have advanced in race relationships in this country and in the south, I realized the deep implications of such a proposal. As pastor of a Southern Baptist church which had been geared for forty years to minister to white, middle-class America, I did not know what the outcome would be. I had been at Southside as pastor for less than a year. I could not even predict how the people might respond.

In the days following that first initial discussion of this possible solution, my mind played all sorts of tricks on me. I imagined and dreamed of what could happen. Ministers are human and no matter how deep the dedication and commitment, we think in human terms. And if I were to suggest to a white congregation, even though it was within a predominantly black neighborhood, that they should merge with a black congregation, I did not know whether I would have a visit from the Ku Klux Klan, or a cross burned in my yard, or receive threatening phone calls, or what. If I did respond in the affirmative to this proposal, it indeed would be a challenge to communicate the idea to the people of Southside Baptist Church. It would be an adventure to bring three churches in the unity of spirit necessary to accomplish such a feat.

One of the thoughts that gripped me throughout was that sometimes it is difficult for one Baptist church to work together with unity of purpose and harmony of spirit, but to create a situation where three Southern Baptist congregations are put together to improve a situation would take total unity of purpose, complete harmony and agreement, mutual respect and understanding. This puzzled me. I had made a decision to come to Saint Petersburg, that was difficult for me. I made the decision to stay at Southside Church and in Saint Petersburg after I arrived and studied the situation in-depth. Now I felt the Father calling on me again to venture into the unknown country. And for the first time in my life I had a true sense of what being a pilgrim is all about.

In the days and weeks that followed I wrestled with the simple question: What am I going to do? I was convinced that the church of the Lord Jesus Christ was not called to go out of business. I believed that a church was called on to minister in its neighborhood, in its community. If a church cannot minister to its community, to the people who live within its shadows then it will lose its power and eventually cease to exist. I believed, and I continue to believe, that a church ought to minister to whoever is in its community. I became convinced that as Southside Baptist Church was presently constituted that it could not minister to its community. I felt, therefore, that it was imperative for the congregation of Southside Baptist Church to take decisive action to insure the continuing ministry of this fine church on the south side of Saint Petersburg. I knew that if I entered into such an adventure that it would demand total commitment. It was my feeling and my belief that this was the right thing to do. In my mind and on paper during those days that followed the luncheon, I wrestled with the angels. Finally, I had a sense of belief that this was the most viable alternative. I had examined Tabernacle Baptist Church and my investigation showed that its pastor was a most unusual man and that his church was a most unusual church. Tabernacle Baptist Church was involved in its community. It was active and concerned. It was ministering. It was my belief that if such a merger could take place then the newly merged church could reach the people that surrounded it.

Having made the commitment, with the belief that this was of the Spirit of God, I began the long and tedious preparation of presenting a proposal of this nature to the people of Southside Baptist Church. Dr. Graves, Mr. Guess of the associational office, and myself met and talked through some possible ramifications. We discussed some things that would have to be worked out and some things that would have to be done before it could be finalized. It is very difficult for me at this writing even to try to express how it came about and how it was consummated. I know of no human way to explain it, only a spiritual way. What was to follow as well as what had occurred was an impulse of the Spirit of God. It happened so matter of factly that it is very difficult, almost a year later, to think back on it and put it on paper. When it was happening, I attempted to record my feelings and what was taking place. That was perhaps the hardest thing of the entire situation. To the best of my knowledge, nothing like this has been done within the structure of the Southern Baptist Convention. Churches in transition communities have sold their property to black congregations. They have sold their property to other denominations. They have sold their property to industry and moved to another location. They have refused to sell, refused to deal with the situation, and remained until the church has ceased to exist. The idea of three churches coming together, one black and two white, where one assumed the indebtedness of another, where black and white congregations have come together for worship, to the best of my knowledge was a new event. This was a first. This made it even more difficult since there was no precedent. What follows is what went into making up the reality of this merger. It truly was of God or else it could not have occurred.

Shortly after my meeting with Dr. Graves and Mr. Guess, I met with the attorney for Southside Baptist Church to discuss the legal aspects for such a merger. One of the things that I faced as a young pastor out of seminary was a lack of business administration knowledge. A pastor of a church in a transitional community is called on to serve as a business manager as well as a pastor. During the year I served at Southside, I conferred with attorneys concerning lease agreements, foreclosures, and merger situations. I conferred with bank presidents and other lending institution officers about loans, payments, anticipated action for non-payment, and the like. As pastor of a church I had to reduce a budget, administer that reduced budget, renegotiate loan payments, make interest payments, and the like. Things of this nature are very much a part of the ministry.

Following what I considered to be an understanding of the legal aspects of a merger, I moved on to begin the preparation for the presentation of this merger idea to the Southside Baptist Church. The first Sunday in April, Mr. Bill Guess spoke at our eleven o'clock worship service to show associational support for our church and for the efforts of its pastor. In the same month I scheduled a deacon's retreat and leadership meeting of Southside Church at our associational assembly. I enlarged my study of the past ten years of Southside Baptist Church, prepared flipcharts, overhead projections, along with graphs and charts to reveal in-depth the present situation of Southside and to create awareness on the part of church leadership. Also, I wanted to seek their ideas and to explore possibilities that they might have concerning a solution. Mr. Guess and Mr. Dobbins, of the Florida Baptist Convention, attended the retreat along with myself and those previously mentioned.

We arrived at the assembly around five o'clock in the afternoon.

After dinner we went to our cabin and began to explore our church situation. The discussion, the questions, the searching for answers continued till almost three o'clock in the morning. I think for the first time that night, the deacons of Southside Church finally admitted to themselves the seriousness of our situation. When you have been connected with a church for forty years, it is very difficult to admit that if something is not done within another three to five years the church that you love will be nonexistent. I will long remember that night and the very heavy burden I felt on my shoulders and in my heart.

The next morning around twenty other leaders of our church joined us at the assembly. We began again going over the same materials, the same charts and graphs, making the same projections to all of our leadership. One of my questions was, what can we do? We were at a crossroads, what could we do? We began to explore possibilities of community ministries, of things they felt like we needed to do to reach the community we were in. Further along in the discussion it became apparent that as we were presently constituted we did not have the financial resources nor the strength of leadership to render those ministries. To do what our church leadership suggested, we would have had to increase our budget, which we were not presently meeting; we would have had to place anywhere from three to six more jobs on people who had five jobs within the church already.

But one of the overriding factors that we dared not leave out was that we were a predominantly white congregation in a predominantly black community. There was a lack of understanding of the black culture and the black way of life among our people. For five years a few dedicated people had made a gallant effort to reach out to that neighborhood and community with very little visible results. Taking into consideration the black separatism that we find in our country today, our people decided that they were not sure that we could reach the community. Another factor that they brought to life was that seemingly not all people were willing to have an open congregation. In order to have an open congregation you must have total unconditional love and acceptance. Without this unconditional love and acceptance there cannot be an open congregation.

Following lunch that day, we returned to the cabin and began once again to renew our struggle in an effort to find some solution. It had been the intention of Mr. Guess, Mr. Dobbins, and myself not even to mention the idea of the three-way merger. It seemed however that the situation dictated that we do so. I had been leading the discussion and review of the study that I had made with Mr. Guess and Mr. Dobbins contributing as outside resource people. However, it was Mr. Guess who sensed, I think again at the bidding of God's Spirit, the timing of the hour. Feeling led to do so, and sensing that the people were at that place of wanting and desiring a word of hope, he presented the idea of a three-way merger.

Much to my amazement the leaders of Southside Baptist Church responded in a most open and favorable manner. One thing that we all feared more than anything else, was that the time would come when we would have to close the doors and Southside would cease to exist. If that had been allowed to occur, it would have been a heartbreaking experience.

One of the most gratifying times in all of my life occurred shortly after Mr. Guess had presented his presentation and the initial reaction was favorable. One of the ladies of our church, one of the most dedicated and committed Christians I have ever met, spoke up and said, "Mr. Guess, if we follow through with this proposal, what will happen to our preacher?" She continued, "We felt led of God to call him to be our pastor and what you are proposing really moves him out of the picture. I personally could not be a part of something that would hurt my preacher." Words cannot express, a pen cannot write the feeling that came over me at that moment. Seemingly the gates of heaven opened and God the Father stood in our presence in reality. It seemed as if the burden that I had been carrying for almost a year had been lifted. I had seen the situation. I had evaluated it, I had studied it and now had presented it. All of the tension and anxiety of the past months was now relieved.

I believe in the expression of love that woman gave, I knew that beyond a shadow of a doubt that God had called me to Saint

Petersburg. He had called me there for a task, to lead that church, his people, out of the wilderness. I believe that through his Spirit he had provided the solution. The burden had been lifted from my heart, my shoulders, and from my mind. I finally knew that no matter what happened after this that God was going to work it out. Finally after this feeling came over me, I had to sit down and the only way that I could get relief was to weep. I sat on that front porch of that rustic old cabin on a cool April afternoon and wept like a baby. It wasn't that I was sad or hurt, quite the contrary, I was happy, I was rejoicing. For I saw the moving of God in the lives of his people and in the life of his church. A movement that would pull three Baptist congregations together, to work out a mutual problem without any regard to size, race, or financial condition had begun. That Saturday afternoon will live forever in my mind and in my heart. It was more than an idea that had been born; it was God breaking into our lives to work a work among us.

After our retreat, I met with Mr. Guess. We discussed the merger and evaluated the retreat. I sent a letter to Dr. Grave and the First Baptist Church explaining the results of the retreat I then began to move toward what seemed to be the hand of God moving us in the direction of merger. I contacted the Home Mission Board and Mr. Don Mabry, a consultant in the Metropolitan Missions Department and invited him to Saint Petersburg to meet with me concerning the situation at Southside Church. I proceeded to set up a churchwide meeting to explain the retreat, the purpose of it, and to share with them the same presentation that had been presented at the Baptist assembly.

Mr. Mabry arrived and we spent all day evaluating the situation, looking at the facilities, and discussing the possibility of the three-way merger. I presented to Mr. Mabry the findings of the study. He read the study, made comments on it and evaluated it We listened to tapes that had been made at the retreat an discussed them. At our meeting that night, I shared with our congregation from my heart regarding my call to the ministry and my call to Southside Baptist Church and my belief that the church must minister effectively where it is. I also affirmed them and the past forty years of the Southside Church and the desire for its ministry to continue and never die. I told them the sense of responsibility that I felt as pastor of the church and the responsibility that I had toward providing effective leadership. I shared in detail my personal evaluation of the situation and the findings of the study. They were told of all the meetings and discussions that had gone on with members of our state convention staff, associational staff, Southern Baptist Convention staff, and others. Mr. Mabry shared with the congregation what was happening across the Southern Baptist Convention in situations like the one at Southside. He gave his personal evaluation of the situation and his projection for the future. He led our congregation in a discussion concerning the data that had been presented during the evening. The discussion was healthy, and the atmosphere was one of reserve. Ideas were well received, and there was a great deal of openness among the congregation.

I presented the possible merger proposal, dealing with the three-way merger between First Baptist Church, Tabernacle Baptist Church, and Southside Baptist Church. It was received with openness and a good spirit and really an endorsement. Also attending this meeting was a deacon committee from the First Baptist Church. Following the consummation of the merger, I discussed the meeting with the deacons from First Baptist and they were most impressed with the spirit of the people of Southside.

In the following days, I had another meeting with the attorney for Southside Baptist Church concerning the legal matters of a merger and what requirements we must fulfill. On that same day I met with a group from the First Baptist Church. Later that day I met with the deacons of Southside Church, and the topic of discussion of course was the merger. At this time support and reaffirmation came from the deacons. The same week I received a letter from Mr. Don Mabry evaluating the meeting in a most positive light.

A couple of days later I met with the pastor of the Independent Baptist Church, the church that was leasing the mission property. At that time I notified the pastor that Southside Church would not renew their lease and would expect them to exercise their option to buy the property or to give up the property. Some couple of days later a counteroffer was made by this body. The offer was less than Southside Baptist Church's indebtedness. Of course this created a situation where Southside Baptist Church became responsible for the mortgage payment in excess of nine hundred dollars in addition to our other expenses. We were running from a thousand to two thousand dollars in the red, and now we were facing a nine hundred dollar additional mortgage payment. This situation created an imminent financial crisis.

In May 1975, I met with the various parties involved and a merger proposal was drafted. The following is a copy of the proposal that was presented to Southside Baptist Church.

1. That Southside Baptist Church as presently constituted initiate the following actions:

    A . That Southside Baptist Church request of Tabernacle Baptist Church, 930 Eighteenth Street South, that their congregation merge with Southside Baptist Church, thereby forming the Southside Tabernacle Baptist Church.

    B . That we further request Rev. Lewis Lampley become the pastor of Southside Tabernacle Baptist Church.

    C. That the officers and offices of the newly formed Southside Tabernacle Baptist Church be vacated and new elections held after the merger is completed.

    D. That all members of Southside Baptist Church who wish to be a part of Southside Tabernacle Baptist Church and all

Lewis C. Lampley, William J. Guess (Pinellas Association), Delos L. Sharpton

members of Tabernacle Baptist Church who wish to be a part of Southside Tabernacle Baptist Church be allowed to do so and have equal standing with each other.

E. That the deacons, trustees, and pastor of Southside Baptist Church be given the authority to negotiate the above merger with Tabernacle Baptist Church.

2. We further recommend that Southside Baptist Church request of First Baptist Church, Saint Petersburg:

A. That those members not wishing to remain with Southside Tabernacle Baptist Church be allowed to merge with First Baptist Church.

B. That Rev. Delos Sharpton be employed as a staff member of First Baptist Church.

C. That First Baptist Church assume the total indebtedness of Southside Baptist Church ($69,000).

D. That First Baptist Church receive title to Bay Point property and pastorium.

E. That First Baptist Church seek to establish a ministry center at Bay Point that will best serve the needs of that area. Such ministry center may or may not take on characteristics of a local church.

F. That deacons, trustees, and pastor of Southside Baptist Church be given authority to negotiate terms of above merger.

3. We further recommend that the negotiated terms of the merger of Southside Baptist Church with Tabernacle Baptist Church and Southside Baptist Church with First Baptist Church be presented to the congregation of Southside Baptist Church for its approval.

Following the drafting of this proposal, it was presented to the leadership of Southside Baptist Church, and it was their consensus that it should be presented to the congregation. Adequate notice was given and on May 11, 1975, the proposal was presented to the church. The vote was ninety percent in favor of the proposal. This opened the way for negotiations concerning a possible three-way merger.

Following this vote I sent a letter to the pastor of Tabernacle Baptist Church and the pastor of First Baptist Church notifying them of the results of the proposal. Within several days of the vote of the Southside congregation, I received word that in a business conference Tabernacle Baptist Church had voted in the affirmative to respond to the merger proposal as offered by Southside Baptist Church. The congregational response from Tabernacle Baptist Church is given in the next chapter.

Following the passage of the proposal at Southside Baptist Church and the response from Tabernacle Baptist Church, a joint committee made up of church leaders from Southside Baptist Church and Tabernacle Baptist Church met to begin negotiating the merger. That same week I received a letter from Dr. Jim Graves, pastor of First Baptist Church, Saint Petersburg, stating the intent of their church to move forward on the possibility of a three-way merger. In June of 1975, we tried to bridge the gap between Tabernacle Baptist Church and Southside Baptist Church. A series of joint services were held with pastors rotating the preaching responsibilities in order to create and foster better understanding between the two churches.

During the months of June and July, I had meetings with Dr. Graves and committees of First Baptist Church concerning their position in the areas that needed to be negotiated. The merger committees of Southside and First Baptist Churches met together to go over the proposals and the response from First Baptist Church. Also in June a joint meeting of a committee from Southside Baptist Church and Tabernacle Baptist Church was held to continue the negotiations leading toward a possible merger.

On June 22, 1976, a final proposal for merger was presented to Southside for approval. It was approved. Also that month it became necessary to renegotiate a bank note extension that came due. We had to request deferment of loan payment to the Florida Baptist Convention for at least the month of July and possibly longer. At this time I felt like our people needed a word of encouragement from the participants working for the merger. Dr. Jim Graves, pastor of First Baptist Church, and Lewis Lampley, pastor of Tabernacle Baptist Church sent a letter to the membership of Southside seeking to encourage them during this time of negotiation. These letters were read to the congregation during one of our services.

Throughout these months of negotiation and working out the legal details of merger and waiting for the final response from First Baptist Church, I felt it necessary to devote my attention as much as possible to the sustaining of our congregation. I attempted to gear my sermons to the needs of the people, seeking to pinpoint where we were and what we were doing. My sermons dealt with the mission of the church and the personal responsibility that each Christian has in seeing that the kingdom of God is advanced. I tried to articulate my own feelings and the feelings that we should have as Christians with regard to the work of the Father. This was a most difficult time for the people of Southside Baptist Church. A church which had an outstanding history for over forty years, a church with a very proud position, had to realize that a ministry was not ending when a merger occurred but was being expanded. During these weeks and months of negotiations I tried to express to our people the idea that the kingdom of God is larger than any of us. What matters most is that the kingdom of God advances and not that we get what we want. I think that this was brought very clearly to my conscience following a morning worship service.

I was standing at the front door of our sanctuary following the service, as was my custom, and one of our elderly members came by, grabbed my hand with both of hers, and with tears in her eyes looked at me and said, "Preacher, can't we just stay like we are, we've had such a good time, we love one another. Can't we just stay like we are even though there are just a few of us." Without a doubt one of the hardest things that I have ever had to do was to respond to that lady. She lived in the community, she couldn't move her church membership, and she didn't know if she could adjust to an open congregation. She wanted things to stay just like they were. I looked at her, and I knew that I had to respond. Finally I put my arm around her and said, "No, I'm sorry, we can't. For you see God hasn't asked us to always be comfortable, at ease, but to do his will. You know I'd like for things to stay the way they are, too, but I know we can't. For although we are having a good time one with another, we are not doing what God called us to do." With tears still in her eyes, she said as she looked up at me, "I know, I know, but it sure is hard."

Those were some very difficult days trying to keep people together when you knew that they might soon be broken apart. And I guess what hurt me most was although I knew that this was what God would have me do, I also knew that there would be some of the people who would not stay at the merged church since it would be predominately black. They were unable to move to another church, and so they would be separated from the church altogether. Some of these had been members of the church since it was founded. Now the church as they knew it was no more, and there was nothing to take its place for them. As a pastor that hurt. However, we must realize that the kingdom of God is bigger than any one of us. And whether we live or we die the Father will march on.

A situation such as we were involved in at Southside Baptist Church, Tabernacle Baptist Church, and First Baptist Church always draws attention from those who do not have the correct information. During these days before the merger was finalized the rumor mills were in high gear. So, at my request Mr. Guess, the director of missions for the Pinellas Baptist Association, drafted a memorandum to all the churches in the association explaining the details of the merger. It was my hope that this would quiet some of the rumors and settle some of the people's anxieties. What had dismayed me during this time was the fact that people from fellow churches had approached me, asking me to encourage some of our people at Southside Baptist Church to move their membership to their churches when the merger was completed. The situation was critical enough without having this added anxiety and pressure. I assured those parties that I would not make such a request of any of our people. If the merger was approved, our people would have the freedom to remain, to go to First Baptist Church, or affiliate with a church of their choice. But I would not be the one to encourage our people to go anywhere.

In August of 1975, the membership of First Baptist Church, Saint Petersburg, accepted the proposal for a three-way merger. This lead the way for the consummation of the merger. I met with Lewis Lampley and assisted him in drafting a new constitution and bylaws for the new church. We also appointed a nominating committee for the new church.

Finally, a joint committee was held to finalize the merger. Southside Tabernacle was the name selected for the new church. Thus, bringing the two separate entities, Tabernacle and Southside together. In the end, three Baptist churches, one black, two white had worked together without one setback, one disagreement, one conflict, one instance of angry or harsh words. My earlier fears had no substance. It is my conviction that without God being in it this three-way merger would have failed.

September 7, 1975, was the date set for the dedication service at Southside Tabernacle. Pastors and churches throughout the city along with city officials attended the service. It was a testimony to what God had done.

On September 11, 1975, the final meeting was held to close the merger. Representatives from each church, their attorneys, and representatives from involved financial institutions attended.

The final papers were signed and what was the impulse of the Spirit of God became a reality.

Southside Baptist Church struggled successfully to find how to have an effective ministry in a changing neighborhood. The solution it found may not be "the model" for churches located in a transitional neighborhood but I am convinced it is "a model."

Perhaps Thoreau described the pilgrimage of the people of Southside Baptist Church best when he wrote: "If a man does not keep pace with his companions, perhaps it is because he hears a different drummer. Let him step to the music he hears, however measured or faraway."

NINE

A Curious and Exciting Possibility

"Somewhere, if you'll only listen for it, There is always a voice saying the right thing to you" (Thomas Hughes).

In this brief treatise, I will endeavor to describe the preparation, response, reactions, and the attitudes reflected when, in an unprecedented fashion, a predominantly white Southern Baptist congregation issued a proposal to merge with a predominantly black congregation.

After much painful study and agonizing discussion, Tabernacle Baptist Church, in a special business meeting on Mother's Day, May 10, 1975, initiated the following:

"That Southside Baptist Church request of Tabernacle Baptist Church that their congregation merge with Southside Baptist Church, thereby forming the Southside Tabernacle Baptist Church."

The request was monumental! The congregation received the news with both jubilation and curiosity. "We have prayed for a miracle, but not necessarily in this fashion," someone commented. The miracle alluded to was a place to relocate because the congregation had reached its saturation point. That means we didn't have adequate space for training. To deal with that problem; Sunday School and new believers' classes were meeting in buses, cars, and two departments. The children and youth were meeting in buildings a block away from the main sanctuary.

Because of the lack of funds and little vision, the organizers of Tabernacle Baptist did not provide educational facilities. The lack of a facility could have been problematic, but instead, we turned it into a profitable project by engaging ourselves in fervent prayer and way-of-life evangelism.

Prayer

The needs and nature of our ministry led to the initiation of a twenty-four-hour prayer ministry which involved people for fifteen minutes each Saturday from 6:00 A.M. through 6:00 A.M. Sunday. At times we would pray all night! And as we prayed God gave us favor with many people. In other words, we did what we could and God did those things that we could not do. Prayer then, was the key that prepared us for what God had in mind since eternity past—the merger!

When the idea came to my attention (as I stated earlier), I was intrigued by the possibilities that it projected. Fellowship with white Baptist preachers through the Pinellas Baptist Association had given me the opportunity to develop a camaraderie that was genuine and Christian. The people as a whole were not able to have that opportunity at first. At the beginning, the question naturally arose, what is the hidden meaning of the suggested merger? There must be some strings attached, especially if First Baptist, which is mostly white is assuming a $66,000 mortgage plus a staff salary for the former pastor of Southside.

"Pastor, are you sure that we should do this?" some of the officers were asking.

"This is miraculous," the Holy Spirit assured me. By nature, I am an optimist—so to me, just the thought was good.

Response

After meeting with the deacons, department heads, and the congregation, on May 16, (my birthday) 1975, the congregation by vote responded to Southside's request:

1. "That Tabernacle Baptist Church merge with Southside Baptist Church." Upon the completion of the merger/organization of

the new Southside Tabernacle Baptist Church, we appoint:

a. A constitution and by-laws committee (Pastor Sharpton ex-officio).

b. A Nominating Committee (Pastor Lampley ex-officio). The new elections to take place at least two weeks before both bodies occupy the building . . . in order to orientate, brief, train, and plan together.

2. We further recommend that:

1. Tabernacle Baptist (as presently known) assume the financial responsibility for repairs, renovations, proper office equipment, pastor's study, class rooms, kitchen, dining room, carpeting, and the houses.

2. The two ministers be given the authority to immediately appoint the following committees for inspection and evaluation in terms of needs, and cost:

A. Repair and renovation committee. This committee responsible for the facilities, inside and outside.

B. Beautification Committee. This committee will be responsible for landscaping and paving.

C. Bus Maintenance Committee. This committee will be responsible for painting the buses and getting them in top shape.

3. Monies be spent for materials, supplies, and equipment only. The labor will be done by the men of the church.

4. All the ABOVE BE FINISHED before the occupancy of the new Southside Tabernacle Church, if at all possible.

We further recommend that a transition period be considered (ninety, sixty, or forty-five days) because we need to be considerate and sensitive to God's people who have labored for years in both ministries. Therefore, whatever is comfortable to Southside in any regard needs to be complied with. During this period, we should plan the following:

1. Periodic services together

2. Action . . . for Sunday School enrollment

3. Dedicatory service

4. Budget planning
5. Stewardship emphasis.

During the transitional period between May 10th and August 10th, (Southside's final vote on the merger), we met for discussions, worship services, and special sessions with Rev. William J. Guess, the director of missions for Pinellas Baptist Association. As I reminisce, it is remarkable how we could sense God's hand directing every decision and event.

In the words of Milo H. Gates:

The finest test of character is seen in the amount and

The power of gratitude we have.

We sincerely thank God for allowing us to be a part of such a monumental feat!

Purpose

The question was, how can we provide a more effective ministry?

Churches often sell and relocate. Eventually Tabernacle could have found facilities. Here were two churches, both with mixed congregations, one predominately black, one mostly white, of like faith and order, as we say. It was not just getting someone to occupy the building, it was a blending of faiths, ministries, and cultures.

Delos Sharpton, former pastor of Southside Baptist Church:

"Our desire was to minister to the people. That was the total driving force that we had in mind when we went into this study."

William J. Guess, director of missions for the Pinellas Baptist Association:

"To further undergird our purpose for existing, our future plans involve concerted programs for the elderly, blacks and interracial families, who are faced with all kinds of difficulties; mainly, rejection, and toleration" (Statement to the News Media).

How a Deacon Saw It

The Lord has blessed us with a ministry that is centered around the actual teachings of Christ.

There was actual Bible study being performed . . . different classes to meet different needs: orientation for new believers, reentry for those who had strayed and returned, and pre-baptism sessions for all who were to be baptized. All these ministries posed a problem—the lack of space. It was our goal to build or expand so that we could accommodate the needs of the people.

The Bible points out, "Where there is no vision the people perish." So you see, we were scriptural in setting a goal.

Sometimes we become so goal oriented that we seek to accomplish it without the help and the leading of our Lord and Savior, Jesus Christ. Then there are those who will seek the help of God but will not yield to the answers which he gives. I think more than anything, we as a church fell into this particular category.

We, as a church did seek the help of the Lord in reaching our goal of a new building or a renovation of the old one. We were constantly on our knees praying to God for wisdom and insight. We prayed and it seems as if God was saying wait! But we kept on looking and investigating—praying. But as always the answer that he gave us was contrary to the one that we expected. God quietly said Wait!

In the meantime, we were not aware of the fact that God had been making plans to give us bigger and better things. He was speaking to the hearts of another group of believers to carry out the plans that he had in store for us.

He was speaking to the members of Southside Baptist Church. He was preparing to use them as well as he was preparing to use the members of Tabernacle Baptist Church to reach thousands and thousands of people.

He decided to bring these two congregations together to do something which was unheard of in modern times. God was

Southside Tabernacle leaders: William G. Bryan (deacon), Pastor and Mrs. Lampley, Mark Wolfe (music)

bringing together a predominantly black and a predominantly white congregation into a holy union to accomplish a greater work than either of the congregations ever imagined.

With this act, God was going to answer the prayers of hundreds of people with different racial and ethnic backgrounds. He was helping us as a struggling church in spite of ourselves!

Yes, our God is "able to do exceedingly abundantly above all that we ask or think, according to the power that worketh in us, Unto Him be glory in the church by Christ Jesus throughout all ages, world without end, Amen" (Rohland Bryant, Chairman of Trustees).

Suspense

Most of the community was permeated with suspiciousness and a wait and see attitude. One minister advised, "Watch them closely, preacher." Others would ask, "Lampley, what are you doing?" I would simply reply, "Being obedient to God."

The merger in my opinion, was a supernatural act. To God be the glory!

A Commendation

My hat is off to the First Baptist Church. They demonstrated genuine love and complete trust in our competence. In other words, they did not meddle—they just quietly did what they were committed to doing . . . alleviating the financial burdens.

Not one time did anyone, to my knowledge, call to question or advise us. Surely, this was the doings of God by his Spirit!

Ah, yes, at the beginning, questions naturally arose, "What are the hidden meanings of the proposed merger?"

But with many of our people, I could sense that the idea offered stimulating possibilities for the growth of a congregation that was emerging from obscurity as well as seeking ways to expand its facilities and programs.

New vistas were appearing on the horizon, but as a pastor, I needed to be reminded that renewal was a constant need. In his book *Why Churches Die,* Hollis Green wrote, and I concur, "The success of the harvest depends not only on the soil and the touch of the finger of God, it depends on the husbandman who cares for the growing plant. This seems to be an essential of renewal. When the harvest does come, there may be many workers going into the field to gather fruit.

"Adequacy in this respect usually points back to the leadership and nurturing of a faithful man of God. Revival comes with the sowing of good seed."

I am far within the mark when I say, it is indicative that the churches that were involved were already recipients of spiritual renewal—revival, if you please. Excitement is only valid when it induces incitement!

TEN

The Kingdom Better Understood

Out of the spring meeting between Bill Guess, Delos Sharpton, and Jim Graves, a number of things began to happen. Delos Sharpton faced the involved process of informing his church leadership of the possibilities of the suggestion to merge with Tabernacle and First Baptist Church. An approach was made to Lewis Lampley and then to the leadership of Tabernacle Baptist Church with the basic elements of the suggested merger. A number of discussions between leaders of Southside and Tabernacle ensued. Then, a point was reached in which both of these churches were of the opinion that the merger had, indeed, great potential.

As the leaders of Southside and Tabernacle progressed in their discussions, a formal request was made of First Baptist Church by the two other churches for participation in the merger. Though the preliminary idea was born in a discussion with the pastor of First Baptist Church, it was concluded from the beginning that the merger could not be successful unless all action taken originated with the two churches since they were more directly involved. Until the more formal request was made, the leadership of First Baptist Church had very little awareness of the proposal. The pastor had discussed the possibility with the chairman of deacons, but the deacons had not taken the matter into consideration.

Upon presentation to the deacons by the pastor, a small ad hoc committee was appointed to study the proposal and report back to the deacons. Probably the most meaningful action taken by the committee was a visit to Southside Baptist Church in which the proposed merger was discussed in an open church session. The men later related the deep emotion that they had experienced as they witnessed this church agonizing over the responsibility to their community and to their Lord and to the faithful members of that church who had built a fine ministry through the years. The men discovered firsthand that the request was made not only out of some desperation in a financial crisis, but also out of dedication that the ministry of some forty years in that community continue in the years ahead.

As the discussions developed with First Baptist Church concerning the proposed merger, most considerations involving First Church had to do with Southside rather than Tabernacle. The responsibility of First Church would involve three primary factors. The first was that First Church would assume the responsibility for the indebtedness of Southside Church. Upon closer study the ad hoc committee learned that there was a note with a local commercial bank which needed immediate attention. The major portion of the loan was with a federal savings and loan institution and encumbered the property of Southside Church as well as a mission site which they had purchased. A third loan had been secured from the Florida Baptist Convention and several thousand dollars was still outstanding. In addition to these mortgage obligations, serious operating deficiencies were being faced by the Southside Baptist Church which added pressure to accomplish something as soon as possible.

The second matter concerned the future of Delos Sharpton, the pastor of Southside Church. Though some effort to assure his future had been discussed from the beginning, an added dimension for the ad hoc committee was the sincere concern of the Southside members for the security of their young pastor. Very early in the conversations, the ad hoc committee came to share a strong conviction that whatever else happened, action should be taken that would be helpful and supportive to Delos Sharpton.

The most viable possibility for the future of the Southside pastor was for him to become an assistant pastor of First Baptist Church.

The third matter had to do with an unanticipated factor. In the preliminary discussions of the leadership of Southside Church, a strong feeling developed that the pastorium in which Delos Sharpton lived should be deeded to First Baptist Church. The strong feeling was due to a conviction that had to do with genuine concern for the pastor. However, there was also concern that the house was located in a predominately white neighborhood some distance from the church. An anxiety reflective of the lack of understanding at the outset of the discussions centered on the possibility of the proposed merged church owning the house in that neighborhood. Another piece of property owned by the Southside Church was a matter of concern. The nearly four acres of land was located in the same extreme southern part of Saint Petersburg as the pastorium. It had been purchased as a potential mission site several years previously. For some seven years the attempts at initiating a mission met with different problems and there seemed to be little promise of a self-sustaining work in that location.

The First Church committee sensed the dual concern of the Southside leaders concerning the mission site. Foremost was a sense of mission and a commitment to this location. They felt some frustration that the mission had not been constituted as a church. They sought assurance from First Church that serious study and effort would be directed toward a meaningful ministry in that location. There was evident also some concern as to long-range use and public opinion if they were to allow the property to continue as the responsibility of the predominately black, merged fellowship. These apprehensions exposed the rather human side of those involved in the discussions of the merger. Such feelings arose out of a lack of understanding between the principals of the merger.

The ad hoc committee of the deacons met with a committee of

the Southside Church to discuss the proposals set out above. Prejudice and suspicion is not confined to race and there was the necessity of some dialogue to effect trust and communication between the representatives of these two churches. First Church is made up of a wide range of socioeconomic groups from all parts of the city. It is somewhat typical of a First Church in a city the size of Saint Petersburg to have less sophistication than is often assumed by those who would judge it from the outside. However, some members are involved in professional and executive responsibilities and, thus, an ad hoc committee, such as the one under consideration, would reflect some of that character of the church. The Southside Church had a more stratified constituency with more middle-income, blue-collar workers. Evident in the first sessions was a little suspicion as these two groups sought assurance that there was no hidden agenda.

Through these discussions, it was determined that the membership of Southside Church should be encouraged to remain in the new merged fellowship if they felt that they could worship and serve effectively. It was agreed from the beginning that honesty would dictate that all parties face the reality that many of the longtime members of Southside would have some difficulty remaining in the church once it became predominantly black. Therefore, an invitation was to be extended from First Baptist Church for any of the members of Southside who felt the need to move to a fellowship more oriented to their mode of worship and traditions to come and join First Church along with their pastor as he came to join the staff. Even as this proposal was developed it was obvious that a double dilemma would be posed to some of the members of Southside Church. For some of them it was as difficult to think in terms of coming to First Church as staying in the merged, predominantly black fellowship. There was silent agreement simply to accept such differences of spiritual expression and need.

A further matter of some discussion had to do with the ultimate disposition of the mission site in south Saint Petersburg. At one time the Southside congregation had seriously considered utilizing that property for a relocation of their church. They had a zealous missionary concern about this area. The committee of First Church considered the matter from a little more objective viewpoint and weighed carefully the reality that the attempts to establish a mission at that location had proven unsuccessful for some seven years. Thus, the First Church committee pledged only to seek meaningful utilization of the property, but emphasized that if viable ministry could not be effected in that area, the property would be sold. It was felt that integrity demanded that an understanding be reached that did not commit First Church to a perennial sponsorship of a mission that was ineffective.

In regard to the pastorium, which Southside had proposed to deed to First Church, an alternative was developed and suggested to the Southside committee. Since the First Church budget did not have any provision to meet the obligations assumed in taking Delos Sharpton on its staff, it was determined that the sale of the pastorium would produce funds to finance any additional financial responsibilities First Church would be assuming. This proposal was made possible by another event which had occurred in First Church. A member of the church had given to the church a duplex and garage apartment to be used for a furloughing missionary residence. If the pastorium were to be sold prior to the time that Delos Sharpton would leave First Baptist Church, he would be moved to the duplex at no expense to him. Furthermore, First Church would commit itself to making certain improvements in the missionary residence to assure the comfort and convenience of the Sharpton family. This proposal was satisfactory to the Southside pastor and committee.

Progress reports had been made to the deacons for two months. By the time of the July meeting in 1975, both Southside and Tabernacle were moving toward agreement and a readiness to consummate the merger. However, so much of their agreement hinged upon the commitment of First Church that they found it necessary to await the decision of the third partner. When the proposal, with its various implications, was brought to the deacons many questions developed as the involvement of people broadened. Several serious potential obstacles were discussed.

At the very outset of discussion, the committee introduced an issue in which they wanted no misunderstanding. Since the Southside Church was already integrated beyond a token point, it was entirely possible that some of the adult black members of Southside Church might choose to respond to the invitation to come to First Church with their pastor, rather than stay in the merged fellowship. The committee felt that any vote taken by the deacons and then the church should be in full awareness of that potentiality. A somewhat predictable discussion followed with a weighing of the various possibilities to First Church. The routine misapprehensions and fears were expressed. Though the church had several black children in attendance through the bus ministry and some of these children would often return on Sunday evening with their parents, there was some concern about the results of blacks seeking membership. One deacon mentioned that he did not care himself but that if some were to come seeking membership there would be some problems. Then a deacon of several years' service stood and very quietly ended the conversation. He said, "Gentlemen, if in doing this we have a problem, it is probably time that we had a problem." With that focus of spiritual responsibility, there was no more discussion concerning any racial implications to the merger.

The ramifications of the financial commitment of the church were reviewed at length by the deacons. Though at this time the proposal to sell the pastorium had developed and offered a way to meet additional expenses incurred in adding a staff member, there was legitimate apprehension concerning the assumption of some $70,000 obligation. First Church's concern for the indebtedness which was about two hundred and fifty thousand dollars was enough to create no little reluctance toward assuming any more debt. After some discussion the chairman of the ad hoc committee shared how the church had helped other churches and missions in times past. He further challenged the deacons that it was a responsibility of First Church to be a leader and helper to sister Baptist churches. This particular conviction, without a doubt, had much to do with the ultimate decision of the church. Unless a church is responsive to the challenges and opportunities that God opens up to them, there is little way that they can fulfill the role of being a church.

Another question raised in the course of the discussion by the deacons had to do with whether the Tabernacle Church ought to assume a part of the indebtedness as an act of good faith. By that time it had been learned that the Tabernacle Church had several thousand dollars in savings toward the building of new facilities. The committee responded to the question by stating the conviction that such a request could very well abort the entire effort in the appearance that the Southside Church and First Church had an ulterior motive. The role of First Church was defined as a catalyst to effect a rather unusual and unprecedented coalition of two fellowships which could make the work of both more effective.

Somewhat unexpectedly, after a period of discussion, a motion was made to reject the proposal of the committee in response to the request of Southside and Tabernacle Churches. The motion was defeated, but there did not seem to be an inclination to approve the proposal. Thus, a decision on the proposal was postponed until the next month's meeting.

The delay in deciding a recommendation to the church compounded the problems of the Southside Church which, by this time, was facing serious problems in meeting day to day expenses. This dilemma of the Southside Church was related to the deacons and one of the men responded by offering a donation to begin a fund that would help them meet that month's obligations. The spirit manifest in that act was contagious and the deacons voted to recommend to the church that up to six hundred dollars be committed to Southside Church for July and a like amount for August to aid them in the period of time First Church was making a decision. That recommendation was approved by the church and enabled Southside to keep current on the mortgage obligations of the church.

After the deacons' meeting, some of the men asked me how I felt personally about the proposal. They indicated that they had not been able to interpret my personal convictions in the matter. I had attempted to guide the men of the committee and to share input in the formulation of the recommendation, but at the same time not to lead the deacons in a decision. At the next month's meeting the question was put to me in the presence of the deacons and I shared a strong conviction that First Church was confronted with a unique opportunity that should not be avoided. For such a venture as this to be completed, I found it necessary to be positive and supportive to the project. Any attempts at neutrality would be interpreted as reluctance or even antagonism to the project.

Another of the concerns that developed during these summer weeks of decision-making was what would be done with the mission site since the committee had indicated that it would not be continued as a mission. A rather vague concept was discussed concerning utilization of the mission site as a satellite of First Baptist Church. The idea had much appeal in that the downtown location offered little space for recreation and day camp programs. Many exciting ideas were proposed for the use of the property in the proposed merger.

In August the deacons voted to recommend to the church that the merger be entered. The recommendation was printed in the church paper as follows:

Deacons Make Recommendation Concerning
Southside Baptist Church

"The Southside Baptist Church of Saint Petersburg has been designated a 'crisis church' by the Home Mission Board due to the changing community where it is located (3647 18 Avenue South).

"In the last decade or so, the surrounding neighborhood of the church has become predominately black. Recognizing the increasing difficulty of ministering effectively to their community, Southside Baptist Church voted May 2 to study a possible merger with Tabernacle Baptist Church, a black Southern Baptist Church, and with First Baptist Church.

"Discussions with Tabernacle Baptist Church have progressed and a tentative agreement has been reached. If this agreement is ratified by both congregations, the Tabernacle fellowship would occupy the present facilities of Southside Baptist Church with a merger of memberships.

"Concurrently with the discussions with Tabernacle Baptist Church, a committee of the Southside Baptist Church has been meeting with a committee of deacons of First Baptist Church, discussing the proposed merger with First Baptist Church.

"After prayerful consideration, the deacons recommend to the church the following action:

1. That the proposal of Southside Baptist Church to merge, in part, with First Baptist Church be accepted with the following provisions:
    1) That all members of Southside Baptist desiring membership in First Baptist Church be received warmly into fellowship.
    2) The debt liability of Southside Baptist Church in the amount of $65,878, be assumed for repayment. (Loans are with a local savings and loan, two commercial banks and the Florida Baptist Convention.)

Southside Tabernacle staff: Richard Jackson (assistant pastor), Ruby Aires (secretary), Pastor Lampley, Richard Lawson (custodian), Rosemary Lawson (day camp), Phyliss Sherrod (organist)

3) The deeds for the church pastorium at 1200 63 Avenue South, and the mission property at 2175 Pinellas Point Drive South, be accepted to become assets of First Baptist Church. The house is appraised at $33,000 and the mission property at $92,000. (The church property on 18 Avenue South would be deeded to the church that results from the merger of Southside and Tabernacle Baptist Churches, with responsibility for insurance and upkeep to be assumed by that fellowship.)

4) That the pastor, Delos Sharpton, of Southside Baptist Church be called as assistant pastor of First Baptist Church.

2. That the pastorium, located at 1200 63 Avenue South, received in the merger with Southside Baptist Church, be sold with the following provisions:

1) The house be sold at the best possible price.

2) The proceeds from the sale of the house be designated to pay the salary of Mr. Sharpton for one year, or until he is called to another church; for the amortization of the loans mentioned above; and for the maintenance of the property at 2175 Pinellas Point.

3) That the immediate operating capital be funded through a loan against the property, subject to the sale of the property.

4) Mr. Sharpton and his family be moved to the mission house of First Baptist Church at 1225 Second Street North.

3. That the property located at 2175 Pinellas Point Drive South, be operated as a satellite for at least a year with the following understanding:

1) It will not be programmed to a typical mission or preaching point.

2) It will be primarily a ministry center and Bible teaching point.

3) It will be used for an extension of regular church programs of First Baptist Church.
4) It will be utilized to minister to people in the area with the expressed purpose of enlistment in First Baptist Church.
5) Communication with the Home Mission Board will be maintained for consultation in the project.
6) After one year, an evaluation of the satellite approach at that location will be made and a recommendation from the deacons be made to the church concerning future operation."

Many details immediately pressed for attention. Arrangements were made at the savings and loan for a transfer of the mortgage commitment of Southside Church to First Church. The church had a very favorable interest rate so efforts were directed toward a simple transfer of the note to the name of First Church. One complication in this procedure was the fact that the mortgage encumbered the church property as well as the mission site. Though the mission site had a value to justify the loan, the savings and loan insisted upon retaining the encumbrance on the Southside property or transferring it to property of the First Church. Such a transfer would have entailed some additional expense, plus some concern was expressed by the institution holding the existing note of the First Church. So the Southside and the Tabernacle leaderships were asked to allow the encumbrance to remain on the entire property until disposition was made of the part deeded to First Church. The subsequent agreement reflected in large measure the degree of mutual trust that had developed through the weeks of discussion. The encumbrance on the property of Southside would complicate efforts to secure additional finances if needed by the merged fellowship. Also, the fact that the church property was dependent upon First Church discharging its responsibility made the agreement one of trust on the part of the merged fellowship. That trust was no small reward for the involvement of First Church.

Now, First Church was faced with the reality that an additional staff member would soon be added with no budget allowance for him. Furthermore, the income level of the church did not warrant such additional expenditure, even though the church had committed itself to help a sister church. It was decided that the most effective thing to do was to put the pastorium on the market for sale to cover all expenses incurred in adding Delos Sharpton to the staff. Once that decision had been made, a loan was negotiated with another commercial bank against the anticipated sale of the house. This loan for twenty-five thousand dollars was then an account from which funds could be drawn for the paying of the note Southside Church had with a commercial bank, and out of which payments could be made on the loan from the Florida Baptist Convention. A moratorium on the payments to the Convention was granted for six months to enable First Church to arrange the means for discharging these new obligations. And the loan in anticipation of the sale of the pastorium afforded a resource for remuneration of the Southside pastor who was made an assistant pastor of First Church.

A commitment was made by First Church to explore for up to a year the possibilities of operating the mission site as a satellite with a review of the matter within a year. On the basis of that proposal it was determined that no long-range financial plans would be made until the decision concerning the satellite had been made. Thus, the first year of operation was secured, but an obvious time of reckoning was to be faced at the end of one year.

A date had been set for the merging of the two fellowships which would continue to meet in the facilities of Southside Church. A date was determined when Delos Sharpton would become a member of the staff of First Church. In the interim Southside and Tabernacle were having joint services and moving toward the consummation of the plan. At the same time, the members of Southside Church were invited to come to First Church as their pastor was invited to preach in that pulpit in anticipation of his joining that staff. Such sharing services helped to alleviate much of the anxiety the people of Southside had concerning the future of their beloved young pastor.

A date was selected when those members that wanted to accompany their pastor to First Church would do so. A very cordial and effective approach was made by the pastor of Tabernacle to the membership of Southside and therefore gave Southside an opportunity to minister before making a decision to leave.

The following letter from the pastor of First Church was mailed to every member of Southside Church extending a welcome to the downtown church but encouraging them to consider staying with the merged fellowship to help make it work:

Dear Friend in Christ:

These recent months have been difficult for you, I know, as you have faced the many problems confronting your church. You are to be commended for your spiritual sensitivity in assuring for the future a vital ministry to the neighborhood you have served so effectively these four decades.

However, change always brings a sadness of parting with the past along with an excitement for the future. Please be assured of the sympathetic understanding and the prayerful interest of all of us at First Baptist. We want so much to be of encouragement and support to you through the days ahead.

From the first mention of your proposed merger, First Baptist has sought the leadership of God in determining how to relate to your need in the most helpful manner. Our concern was to aid in extending your witness in the best way possible and at the same time undergird Tabernacle Baptist Church. Our joint venture has accomplished this purpose, I do believe. Now, we want to encourage you to find that church home where you can and will happily go and serve your Lord. If God leads you to stay with the

Tabernacle-Southside fellowship, we are confident you are facing an exciting and productive era in your Christian life. We want you to know that First Baptist Church extends a warm and genuine invitation to you to join with us.

Please know that we are praying for you in these next weeks as personal decisions are made in the face of church decisions which have been finalized. I look forward to welcoming many of you into our fellowship.

Sincerely,

Jim Graves

About two weeks after the merger was effected, some ten members of Southside Church were received into the fellowship of First Baptist Church along with their pastor. Several others came in the months that followed, but most of them made the choice to stay with the Southside-Tabernacle fellowship. A few moved to churches nearer their homes.

Due to the death of my father, I was unable to attend the joint meeting in September, 1975, when Southside-Tabernacle Baptist Church was constituted. Those members from First Baptist Church who attended the afternoon service of dedication were deeply moved by the experience. There was a spirit of brotherhood and a confidence of victory much in evidence that day. The long anticipated and much discussed merger was at last a reality.

First Baptist Church shared a spiritual experience through the deliberations and the consummation of the merger with Southside and Tabernacle. A missionary vision was rekindled that caused the membership to see not only world missions as an obligation, or a ministry to people of special needs as opportunity, or maintaining a vital downtown fellowship a challenge, but also sensitivity to the problems of sister churches as a mission. The merger served to help create better understanding with other people with different backgrounds and different needs. An enlarged understanding of the role of the church in the modern world resulted. The kingdom was, indeed, better understood.

ELEVEN

The Kingdom Goes On

It is man's nature to fight to the last breath for survival. The same is true for a church in a transitional neighborhood. The members of such a church have invested their lives in the ministry of their church. Some members at Southside Church had given forty years of their lives in commitment and dedication to the cause of the kingdom at this one location. These people may finally acknowledge that the church is located in a changing neighborhood but it is most difficult for them to admit the church they have loved through the years may have to go out of business. Part of the problem in facing this kind of situation is not only the time and energy that has been invested but also the idea that as a people, individually and corporately they have failed. It is part of our American culture to be success-oriented, even in our churches. The statistics of a church in a changing community reflect a failing situation, and this is most difficult to cope with.

Southside Baptist Church asked itself the same question that surfaces in any church that is facing a changing neighborhood. What happened to our leaders? Why can't we find enough workers? Where are all the children and young people? How long will our people drive thirty or forty minutes in order to attend church here? Why can't we reach the neighborhood? What are we going to do? Soon a church in a changing neighborhood must answer some hard and decisive questions. Do we stay? Do we move? Do we sell out and try to start over? Do we dissolve our church? These are not intellectual questions, these are life-and-death questions as far as a church in a changing neighborhood is concerned.

The answers to these survival questions must finally be answered in terms of people. The church is called on to minister to the needs of people. The ministry of the church must minister to the total man. For over forty years, Southside Baptist Church had ministered to the total man. Now with the changing neighborhood, this was not happening. The church had lost identity with its neighborhood. It became a question of facing up to the standards of ministry set up in the biblical revelation. Southside Church like so many others in changing neighborhoods found itself unable to minister to the people of its neighborhood in accordance with these standards. One of the most difficult tasks faced by myself or any pastor of a church in a changing neighborhood is communicating to the people, the encompassing scope of the ministry of the church. It is not enough that we are comfortable and enjoy the fellowship of one another. To be God's church we must live up to the standards he has set for us. He has called his people to be his witnesses throughout the world, and the place to begin doing that is in the neighborhood which surrounds the local church.

It was this belief and conviction that led the membership of Southside Baptist Church to see the three-way merger as an effective way of continuing the long and glorious Christ-centered ministry of Southside Baptist Church. In order to do this the people had to have a vision. The writer of the book of Proverbs said: "Where there is no vision, the people perish" (29:18, KJV). Because the people of Southside Baptist Church had a vision and responded with love, commitment, and courage, their contributions to the kingdom will never perish. The merger with First Baptist and Tabernacle was not the end but the beginning for they had eyes to see what the Spirit of God was doing in their midst.

For the rest of my ministry and the rest of my life, I shall remember the people of Southside Baptist Church for their commitment to the kingdom of God and the sweet spirit which filled their lives and our church. They faced a problem situation and responded with human sacrifice, love, dedication, and courage. They placed the kingdom of God over their own wants and desires. They welcomed a young pastor with love and accepted his leadership. They responded to an idea of merging their church with a black congregation in order to reach a black neighborhood. They placed the ongoing kingdom of God above all. They gave up all to follow the Father, and this is total commitment.

Because of them the past and the future of their church is secure. What was once an aggressive, outreaching church will be again. What once was termed a successful church will be again. What once was a beautiful building, a testimony to the Father, will be again. They found through the merger an effective way for their investment to continue.

TWELVE

The Kingdom More Visible

"The kingdom of God is not meat and drink; but righteousness, and peace, and joy in the Holy Ghost" (Rom. 14:17).

Joy! Gladness! Ecstasy! Congratulations! These are just a few of the happy words that characterized the service September 7, 1975, when the merger was consummated.

The 450 seat sanctuary was filled to capacity and more—as people, black and white, from many walks of life, witnessed and participated in the historical occurrence.

The most electrifying moment came when we responsively recited the "Vows of Commitment." The service began thusly:

Pastor: Believing that the hand of God has led us in planning and uniting the fellowship of these bodies, with gratitude for the past and hope for the future, let us unite in offering ourselves to Him for His honor and glory,

People: We commit ourselves.

Pastor: For the assembling together of the people for the worship of Almighty God, and for the proclamation of the gospel to the lost,

People: We commit ourselves.

Pastor: For the comfort of all who mourn; for the strength of those who are tempted; and for the light of those who seek the way,

People: We commit ourselves.

Pastor: For the conversion of sinners; for the promotion of righteousness; and for the extension of the kingdom of God to the end of the earth,

People: We commit ourselves.

Pastor: For the observance of the ordinances, in the unity of the faith; with charity and good will toward all men,

People: We commit ourselves.

All: To the glory of God the Father, to the honor of Jesus Christ, his only begotten Son, our Savior, and to the praise of the Holy Spirit, our comforter and guide, we make this vow.

The program carried the following significant statement:

"The purpose of these mergers is to provide the best possible ministry in the name of our Lord to the city of Saint Petersburg, Florida. These congregations are grateful to God for his having led us on this pilgrimage toward effective ministry."

The coming together of these congregations was a demonstration of what many sincere Christians yearn to see and experience.

Long before the actualization of the merger, another pastor in the Pinellas Baptist Association, who happens to be black, developed a concept which he calls the "Third Polarization." He points out the fact that "The Third Polarization" is a philosophy (any system of motivating concepts or principles—a basic theory, viewpoint. The system of values by which one lives). "The Third Polarization" recognized the current polarization of Christians along racial lines.

The most obvious example is separate places of worship. The less obvious example is how Christians align themselves on various issues.

"The Third Polarization" further recognized the fact that in America, we are dealing with two cultures, black and white, and if there is to be a Third Polarization of Christians, there must be a real integration of cultures.

If there is to be a true and meaningful integration of cultures, there must be:

1. The recognition of two cultures.
2. A willingness to learn the true values of each culture.
3. An appreciation of the other culture.
4. And, an acceptance of the other culture.

The Third Polarization firmly believes that the uniting of all Christians is essential to the fulfillment of Jesus' prayer in John 17:11 where he prayed saying, "That they may be one, even as we are."

The idea of "The Third Polarization" goes beyond just the integration of and polarizing of Christians of different races. The Third Polarization seeks to bring into realization an atmosphere where all believers can share together as coequals—black and white, rich and poor, learned and unlearned (Mac J. Williams, Sr., Pastor, Mt. Carmel Baptist Church, Clearwater, Florida).

The merger was the beginning of that pastor's dream. For former Tabernacians, it was a confirmation and attestation that we had been right all along in regards to the conviction that in Christ—There is neither Jew nor Greek, there is neither bond nor free, there is neither male nor female: For ye are all one in Christ Jesus (Gal. 3:28).

The new congregation has been able to experience a sincere effort for fellowship and community effort and at the same time, offer a witness to the community at large that through Jesus Christ many things could be accomplished that had long since been considered impossible.

The following testimony lifts up and gives credibility to the hopes and aspirations of a new polarization:

"In June, 1975, I, Rosemary Lawson, age 27, was faced with a difficult situation. The church to which I belonged was falling apart. The end came when the church voted to merge with a black congregation.

I could see my friends, my loved ones in Christ, leaving. To be quite frank, I was afraid that my family would be left all alone in a strange congregation.

I was very wrong and my fears came to an end as old friends left, new ones took their places and the church was still just as much a part of me and I of it, as ever before.

Oh yes, I almost forgot, the pastor is black, which makes not the least bit of difference to me, for as I was crushed with a heavy burden, he took the time to help me find important answers that would affect my entire Christian life.

You see, as a child, I was supposedly saved. But this was not true. I had merely prayed a prayer to stay out of hell, but deep in my heart, I did not believe that God was so great or that I was all that bad; but, I was baptized and called a Christian. At the age of twenty, I prayed a prayer with a heart that was broken and humble; a heart that knew I was rotten through and through; a heart that was truly sorry for all the bad, and really desired to change. Jesus, at that time, came into my heart, and did indeed change my whole life.

Getting right with God was only a first step. Then I had to shape up and get right with my family. Instead of sharing my feelings, I kept them bottled up inside without expression. If I was hurt, I was all alone, even to the point of making myself sick with severe stomach cramps. I did not realize that this made my family feel insecure and unloved by me. Through Bible study and personal counseling with Pastor Lampley, I am now able to openly express myself in a constructive way.

There are yet many problems, heartbreak and discouragement still to come along this road of life, but I also have the wonderful assurance that God is right there, waiting to carry me through, along with my beloved husband by my side, my pastor and church to encourage me all the way.

Therefore, my prayer for Southside Tabernacle Baptist Church and for the loving, giving, understanding man of God that I have found in Pastor Lampley is: "Thank you, Lord, for making my life fuller and more meaningful through my church and pastor."

P.S. Now that I have found a greater, closer walk with my God, I am ready to do God's work. No, that's not right, I really meant that I am ready and available for God to use me to do his work. That work, I feel, is a full-time ministry in the field of children's ministries. As I continue to ask God if this is what he really wants, he continues to answer, "Yes." Where, when or how, I do not know (Rosemary H. Lawson).

The metamorphosis that took place in that young woman and her family is but an example of what is happening throughout the community. Through the courage and commitment of the interracial congregation, the kingdom is becoming more visible to the total community.

THIRTEEN

An Expanded Sense of Mission

As the merger with Southside and Tabernacle was accomplished, First Baptist Church gained an expanded sense of mission. All of the results of the merger are better understood in retrospect since all of the events seemed to be so very natural at the time. There was no real sense of peculiar destiny involved in the decision-making process nor in the implementation of the merger. Yet, as each of us looks back in review of the entire procedure, we are appreciatively gratified at the smooth process by which the merger became reality.

There are several measurable results of the merger in relation to First Baptist Church. The people and the pastor who joined First Church gave that fellowship a better understanding of the trauma of the entire procedure. One of the black members of Southside Church had called during the process of working out all of the details to ascertain if it were possible for her to come to First Church. The assurance she received that she would be welcome along with others from Southside Church seemed to relax some of the anxieties of the move to First Church. Those who chose to come were older members who had given years of service but were no longer able to be actively involved in leadership positions. First Church was able to provide a meaningful fellowship for these people. They became an integral part of the life of First Baptist Church.

The continuing tie of the people who came to be a part of First Church with the friends that they had left behind was demonstrated some months after the merger. I was called upon to lead the memorial services for a lady who had been confined to a nursing home for several years prior to her death. Due to her infirmity she was unable to participate in the merger. One of the families who transferred membership to First Church had ministered to this woman and her sister for several years during her confinement in the nursing home. Because of their continuing ministry after the merger the sisters felt a part of the fellowship of First Baptist Church.

The merger has left First Church with a keen interest in the work and continuing progress of Southside Tabernacle Baptist Church. The kinship that developed between the laity of all three churches gives to both congregations a sense of belonging to each other. Pride and satisfaction were sensed a little over a year after the merger when the Pinellas Baptist Association held one of its annual sessions in the buildings which the Southside Tabernacle Church occupies. The cordial hospitality and testimony of spiritual progress assured all those involved that this really was the result of an impulse of the Spirit.

When First Church converted the addressing system of its weekly mailout to computerized labels, the equipment which had been used was given to Southside Tabernacle Church. Though some inquiry had been made concerning the purchasing of the equipment by another church, leaders in First Church determined Southside Tabernacle should have first refusal of the equipment as a gift before it would be sold. A very supportive attitude developed on the part of First Church toward Southside Tabernacle Church.

A factor which continues to bear positive witness in the community is the manner in which Southside Tabernacle Church has maintained its property. One of the myths which the merger has helped to disprove is that property that comes under the control of blacks will automatically and inevitably deteriorate in appearance and value. This particular myth had risen to the surface several years earlier when a black evangelist came to Saint

Petersburg for a crusade and was jointly sponsored by churches of all faiths. Some of the Baptist churches along with those of other denominations did not participate because of some discussions which took place in the planning sessions of the crusade.

In one particular session the black evangelist was asked if he would involve race in his messages. He indicated that he very well might suggest that as a black family moved into a white neighborhood, that Christians might have great opportunity to witness by befriending them rather than offering their property for sale. To this statement an inquiry was made concerning whether the evangelist would in like manner tell the black people to be responsible property owners and take care of their homes and yards. The evangelist indicated that he would not deal with that situation in the same kind of manner because it would erroneously suggest that every black resident was irresponsible about his property. The resulting tension reflected a contrasting opinion on the part of the black and white participants.

When the Southside Tabernacle fellowship faced the future after the merger, one of the first things that they did was to address the deteriorated state of the buildings they occupied. During the last couple of years that Southside Baptist Church existed, financial circumstances had mitigated against keeping the buildings in good repair. Thus, by the time of the merger, many critical needs existed. The Tabernacle Church had been saving their money for the provision of new facilities. They dedicated their savings to the renovation of the buildings formerly occupied by the Southside Baptist Church and now the home of the Southside Tabernacle fellowship. The result was the very opposite of what some skeptics predicted. The property was cleaned up, painted and, in general, took on the look of proud ownership and aggressive ministry.

One of the members of First Church who had been reared in another state and who had lived his life with some basic assumptions about blacks would frequently drive by the property on his way to attend First Church. He was very impressed with the new occupants of the facilities and would share with me and others his commendation for the merged fellowship. Such effect of the merger may seem small but when multiplied by a number of people, it can become a contribution to breaking down some barriers in attitudes. Probably no situation so prolongs the inequities experienced by the blacks than the inability to effect true mixing of housing opportunities. Only God knows how this one factor can influence a city.

Another of the meaningful results of the merger to the life of First Baptist Church was the investment in the life of Delos Sharpton. Due to financial challenges, the church had effected a year earlier a reorganization of the staff which had, in effect, eliminated the position of a young assistant. Through a combination of assignments, one position was absorbed by the other four ministers on the staff. Even as that was done the church had expressed a desire to enlarge the staff as soon as possible in order to have another young assistant. This was true because the church had sensed a mission in calling young men who had just finished seminary for a couple of years of in-service training and ministry. Due to the merger, that time had come sooner than anticipated.

Delos Sharpton fit the mold of other young men who had served the church in the past. He was bright, capable, and showed great potential for future ministerial leadership. However, as he came to First Church, he was obviously depressed and weary from the pressing responsibility of leading Southside through a difficult period in its history. Furthermore, he had faced the very trying circumstances of watching a church all but die in spite of all that he could do. There was a period of uncertainty in the negotiations with Tabernacle and then with First when it seemed that the one last hope through merger would never be realized. He had shared the temptation to leave in order to save his own personal feelings and ministry, but out of a strong sense of leadership of the Spirit he had determined to see the project through to completion. To his credit Sharpton had remained steady and stable throughout the consideration. Without his leadership, the merger would not have been effected. Nonetheless, as he came to First Church, the strain of that long summer had taken its toll. Thus, the church sensed an additional challenge in the life of this young minister and his family.

First Church provided a nurturing fellowship for the Sharptons. They quickly responded to love and encouragement. Every assignment given to him was discharged with effectiveness. His preaching was warmly received by the fellowship of First Baptist Church and this was no small affirmation to him. The members of First Church derived a real blessing out of ministering to this young family and at the same time his contribution to the life of the church was invaluable.

There was some apprehension on my part at the beginning concerning the attitude Sharpton might have in moving to First Church. Not knowing the young man very well, the thought occurred that he might have difficulty adjusting to the leadership of a senior pastor. Furthermore, the problems of adapting to the role of an assistant minister after having served as pastor were weighed carefully. It was obvious that the move would not be easy. At the same time, any pastor is careful and cautious about just what man is added to his staff. There was a feeling of necessity that the relationship be carefully defined as a staff position not unlike that of a young man called directly from the seminary as opposed to that of a co-pastor. Later conversations between us reflected a shared tension in those early weeks and months of negotiations. However, to me one of the finest effects and most appreciated blessings was that of gaining the friendship of this very capable minister by the name of Delos Sharpton.

Due to the strain of the budget at Southside during the last year prior to the merger, their pastor had not received needed increases in remuneration. A couple of months after the merger, he was given an increase of about two thousand dollars. In spite of the financial situation faced by First Church in which there was no budgeted support for the new assistant pastor, the raise was enthusiastically approved. There was a consensus that the Lord would lead this fine minister to another church and that his compensation should be adjusted as a challenge to any other church considering him to give him adequate financial support. The raise in salary proved to be a helpful encouragement. Furthermore, facing this need of the newest staff member confirmed the church's sensitivity to the other staff members. Some months after the merger was effected, a motion was suggested in a deacons' meeting to make the position filled by Delos Sharpton a part of the staff structure and budget. The discussion that followed reflected a thorough acceptance of Sharpton, but a firm commitment to the course accepted at the outset to let the Lord lead him in the development of his ministry. The same relationship was continued with the assurance that he could stay at First Church as long as he desired. However, he was also assured that he had the support of the church in any move he felt the Lord directed him to make. That action confirmed his acceptance to his new church and gave Sharpton confidence to minister effectively.

As the time ultimately came that he sensed the call of God to accept the call of the First Baptist Church of Donalsonville, Georgia, it was with sincere regret that First Church received his resignation. The merger had afforded First Church another opportunity to experience the reality that staff members are not only called to minister through the church but to be ministered unto by the church. That is a most fortunate expanded sense of mission for any church to realize.

Throughout the discussions concerning the merger, First Church almost exclusively was involved with Southside Church. Though the action of First Church would involve Tabernacle Church indirectly, still it related directly to Southside. Consequently, I had fewer dealings and less dialogue with Lewis Lampley than Delos Sharpton. Nonetheless, an indelible effect of the transaction was a deepening of understanding and appreciation for this very fine black minister. The openness and Christian grace with which Lampley approached each new question or challenge was, without a doubt, critically important to the success of the venture. A lasting result of the merger for First Baptist Church is a greater confidence in Lewis Lampley. Because of the relationship which developed with Lampley, other opportunities for the white and black communities to cooperate in ventures led by their mutual Lord will have more ready acceptance. Such work will give to any church an expanded sense of mission.

Still another strategic factor in the aftermath of the merger for First Church had to do with the property which had been received in the transaction. The pastorium in which the Sharptons lived was placed on the market for sale immediately after the merger was completed. A loan was secured from a local bank against the anticipated sale and the proceeds of the loan financed the responsibility the church had assumed in adding the Southside pastor to the staff. Also, it was determined that expenses incurred in improving the mission site would be charged to that same account. Since a sale of the pastorium would necessitate moving the Sharpton family into the mission house of First Church, there was a general hope that the house would not sell too quickly. The house was on the market for nearly a year with very few seriously interested prospective buyers. However, within weeks after the Sharptons had moved to Georgia, the house sold for very close to the original listed price. Again, there was a confirmation that the experience had been the following of an impulse of the Spirit.

The mission site obtained in the merger offered a different set of problems and opportunities. Since there had been a seven-year history of failure as a mission, First Church had determined from the beginning to seek some other utilization of the property than that of a traditional mission. Interestingly, simultaneous to the consummation of the merger with Southside and Tabernacle, the mission sponsored by Southside came to a crisis time and dissolved. Several of the families in the mission moved their membership to First Church expressing a desire for a church program that offered more for the entire family than the mission could afford. The needs felt and expressed by these families were represented as being generally true of the families that lived in the area of the mission property. Thus, the attitude of these new families in the church confirmed the intent of the church to seek a program other than that of a continuing preaching point for the mission site.

A great deal of interest was developed for the operation of the mission site as a satellite. Plans were discussed for using the property as a recreation site for the downtown church. Experiments were conducted involving a Saturday morning flag football league for the RA's. Several units in the church, such as Sunday School classes and departments, mission groups, etc., used the location for meetings and dinners. The deacons held a monthly meeting there to review the facility and brainstorm the idea of a satellite program. Several work days for the men of the church were scheduled and the buildings and the grounds were made more attractive.

Interest was expressed in a day-care center in the satellite location. A great deal of effort had been given to effect a day-care center in the downtown location with no success. Building code restrictions and limited recreational space had forestalled all efforts toward gaining clearance for a downtown day-care. A study was conducted of the possibility of transporting children from the downtown location to the satellite but this proved undesirable. In the process of evaluating the satellite operation, four years of frustration were ended when the church received clearance to open a day-care center at the downtown location. This new possibility minimized the need for a day-care center at the satellite, and added to the responsibilities of the downtown ministry. The timing of these events contributed to the decision not to operate the satellite in the long-range future.

Still other ideas such as a mature adult center with an extension of the continuing education program of the downtown location were discussed. Bible classes during weekdays for various age groups were considered viable possibilities. A counseling office was suggested as a meaningful ministry in the satellite location. A day camp program in the summer offered exciting possibilities. Many of these ideas will be considered again in another day when great priority can be given to a satellite operation. It is truly an exciting potential extension of a downtown church's ministry.

Yet, problems were faced with the location being in the extreme southern part of Saint Petersburg. Church members who lived in the northern extremities of the city found that the travel time involved to participate in the functions at the mission site made it undesirable. Upon inquiry into the experience and purpose of other churches seeking to develop the satellite concept, it was learned that virtually all who had gone into the program did so as a first step toward relocation. The potential of relocation was no small factor in the success of effective satellite operations. Since First Church had confirmed its intent to stay downtown, there was no long-range appeal for relocation to the property.

Also, the more thought that was given to operating the mission site as a satellite, the more obvious it was that considerably more investment would be necessary. The seventy thousand dollar obligation assumed in the merger was now growing weekly. Even though it was known that the sale of the house would offset some of the expense of the merger, the $25,000 advance on the anticipated sale of the house was quickly disappearing. No long-range plans had been made to take care of the seventy thousand dollar debt, let alone any additional expenditures for improvements to the satellite. The financial considerations of a satellite operation more and more cast a shadow over future possibilities.

In the meantime, continuing reflection and study about the future of First Church confirmed again the necessity of acquiring more property in the downtown location. It was generally conceded that without more property, First Church would eventually die or be faced with the necessity of moving. A strong conviction that the church was where God would have it to be underscored the challenge to secure additional land adjacent to its present location. The only land available was that of the hotel which the church had considered purchasing at an earlier date. The prospects of facing the necessity of additional property downtown coupled with the other financial considerations made it practically impossible to think aggressively in terms of developing the mission site as a satellite. Still, the church had committed itself to explore different possibilities so no action was taken.

During the fall months following the merger, the various experiments seeking to develop the satellite were taking place. Several inquiries were received from potential buyers and they were told that the property was not on the market. The real estate agents representing these parties were told that if their clients were interested they could submit a bid on the property and it would be given fair consideration. Upon such a suggestion the realtors would consistently inquire as to a price. Since the church had made no decision to sell the site, no price had been set, so none could be given. The fact that a piece of land is not listed on the market and that no price is set, makes it extremely difficult to sell. Yet, the church had determined not to list the property until approximately a year after the property had been acquired.

Some six months after the merger, a real estate agent approached the church with the inquiry of a client. Again, he was told that a price had not been set. He indicated he was going to suggest to his clients that they offer a certain amount. Though their offer was somewhat less than his suggestion it was still slightly in excess of the value that had been estimated for the property. The prospective buyer was a church group facing the necessity of relocation and the mission site served their needs admirably. Thus, the opportunity to sell the property and meet all the financial obligations was presented. Furthermore, the property would continue as a viable church facility in keeping with the long-range hopes of the people of Southside Baptist Church. Through several months of negotiations, the decision was reached to dispose of the mission site.

With the sale of the mission site and subsequent sale of the pastorium, First Church found itself in the position to meet all financial obligations incurred in the merger and have a residue of nearly forty thousand dollars. After all expenses were discharged the church voted that all monies remaining would be dedicated to mission causes. Since that time, a minibus has been purchased to be used primarily in the ministry with the deaf, but also to be utilized in other mission ventures of the church as well. Five thousand dollars was sent to the Pinellas Baptist Association office building fund. The rest of the money is in a trust fund to be used as special mission needs are presented.

By the time the sale of the mission site was completed, the prospect of purchasing the hotel adjacent to the church was becoming very probable. The mission fund has been carefully managed in a strong sense that a special opportunity of ministry will be opened up through the future acquisition of the hotel.

What had been entered as a venture of faith had now become a profit. This experience was an affirmation to the membership of First Church. With some apprehension concerning the financial commitment, the church had entered the agreement to participate in the merger. Now, a short year later, a young man's ministry had been salvaged and strengthened, two churches had discovered a means for increased effectiveness, and First Church had received unanticipated funds with which to minister.

Here again, that the impulse of the Spirit had been the original cause of the venture was confirmed. For, about nine months after the merger was effected, I received a call from the owner of the adjacent hotel indicating he was going to sell the hotel and, because of my inquiry and expression of interest, First Church would have the first option to purchase. Many considerations pressed the attention of the church as the proposal was weighed. The owner offered to give the church half the outstanding stock if the church purchased the additional half. With the purchase of the stock a mortgage of some $650,000 would be assumed. In addition, a lease on the land on which the hotel's parking lot was located would have to be assumed. After weeks of study and conversations, and efforts to renegotiate the lease with the owners of the leased portion of the land, a proposal was formulated for presentation to the church. On October 10, 1976, the church voted to purchase the hotel. Though the land is being secured for future expansion, the church has committed itself to operate the hotel as a residence hotel to minister to the many older people who live downtown. The parking lot offers some immediate relief to the parking problem. An air of excitement prevails as First Baptist Church has entered another venture of faith.

More than one member has suggested to me that the positive experience in the merger of Southside and Tabernacle had much to do with the decision to reach out in the purchase of the hotel. God confirmed a conviction in the people of an expanded sense of mission. First Baptist Church is learning the reality of new opportunities in an old situation.

FOURTEEN

A Deeper Sense of Meaning

The people of Southside Baptist Church have given themselves in a sacrificial manner throughout the history of their church. The church had been successful as it advanced from those days in a rented store with wooden crates as pews. The church had made a positive contribution to the life of its community and to the city of Saint Petersburg. One cannot measure the input the ministry of the church had on those individuals with which it had contact. Through the forty-plus-year history many lives were touched and redirected.

The Southside Baptist Church was always a mission-minded church. Even during the days of the changing neighborhood, the people of Southside Baptist Church made missions a priority. Even though the contributions to the church were down, gifts to missions continued with the same consistency as before. In the late sixties, the membership raised enough money to build a Baptist church in Tanzania, Africa. However the greatest mission endeavor on the part of the membership of Southside Baptist Church was not the gifts to Lottie Moon, Annie Armstrong, the Cooperative Program, or the building of a church in Africa: but the merging of their congregation with Tabernacle Baptist Church. This was a great mission venture. It insured the continuing ministry in the surrounding community of which it had been a part for over forty years. To quote Sir Winston Churchill, "This was their finest hour."

The merger gave the people of Southside Church a deeper meaning of what the church is all about. The church is to reach out to the world and not live unto itself. It gave the people a view and exposure to what it means to give so others may know the Father. The people of Southside Baptist Church did not destroy the old but increased its meaning and significance in the community.

Many of the members of Southside Baptist Church continue in serving God at the newly formed Southside Tabernacle Baptist Church. Their vision of aggressive outreach to the church's community continues. Their view and understanding of church membership and ministry has been expanded. Their commitment has entered a new phase of development. Others did not stay to become members of the newly formed church. However, let no one point a finger of judgment at those or any member of Southside Baptist Church. For it was the love of God and commitment to his kingdom on the part of the entire membership of Southside Baptist Church that brought the new ministry to reality.

The Spirit of God moved in the lives of every member during those most difficult days of 1975. The merger agreement and what resulted could not have occurred without the total commitment of the people to do what they felt led of God to do. So today some of the members of the new church were members of Southside Church. Others are members of First Baptist Church, Saint Petersburg, and still others are members of Southern Baptist churches throughout the city. However, regardless of their location, they were and are a great part of what God did in the midst of his people. How else could churches of a different race, and different background come together without conflict and without incident in order to insure that a community would be ministered unto in the name of the Father.

Indeed another chapter has been written in the history of Southside Baptist Church. How shall we evaluate this church and its history? Shall we count it a failure because it was unable to maintain a large membership? Shall we count it a failure because there were periods of decline? Shall we write Southside Baptist Church off as a failure because it is now a predominately black congregation? Shall we count the church as of no consequence because the solution it found to a changing neighborhood was a little different?

How can one count as a failure a church where hundreds of people have made decisions to follow Christ as Lord and Savior? How can a church which has given generously to missions for over forty years be considered a failure? How can a church which has started local mission churches and built churches in Africa be considered a failure? How can a church which experienced times of great spiritual resurgence be considered a failure? How can a church which put the advancement of the kingdom of God ahead of its own personal desires be considered a failure? How can a people which through a personal struggle discovered new meaning to church membership and ministry be considered a failure? How can a people which because of their action insured the continuing ministry of their church be considered a failure?

No, they have not failed when a people have responded to be God's people, called to reconcile the world to the Father. No, they have not failed when they have responded to the contemporary world in a positive and affirmative manner. The people of Southside Baptist Church have remained faithful to their calling to carry on his church and "the gates of hell shall not prevail against it."

FIFTEEN

A Greater Dimension of Ministry

The words of Jesus come into sharp focus here: "The Spirit of the Lord is upon me, because he hath anointed me to preach the gospel to the poor; he hath sent me to heal the brokenhearted, to preach deliverance to the captives, and recovering of sight to the blind, to set at liberty them that are bruised, To preach the acceptable year of the Lord" (Luke 4:18-19).

The amalgamation of the predominately black and the predominately white congregations has captured community attention that heretofore was all but impossible.

The one time predominately black congregation is discovering through the merger and relocation, an opportunity to minister, not only to its own membership, but to a new and enlarged community—a community multiracial in structure, a community defined as "A Crisis Community" in a study prepared by Don Mabry of the Home Mission Board in 1973.

In the study, he stated, "A church may be facing one or more of these transitions: racial, social, economic, housing and/or commercial, and industrial." In the case of Southside Tabernacle, the transition is mostly racial. Poverty also exists, but not hard-core poverty. None of the conditions deterred us, because we are people-oriented.

People! Beings. Human spirits created in the image of God with the ability to love, reason, decide, and hate.

That is what it's all about—people—people capable of hurting and feeling—people who are looked upon as outsiders by casual observers.

The new congregation is discovering effective means of communicating love and concern, and is eliminating many of the prejudices which have been barriers to understanding the total community.

We have found that objectives are essential if we hope to achieve our goals. Our overall objective? To glorify God and to provide a godly atmosphere for all members and visitors, by discipling all available members, and by helping to share God's love and forgiveness with all non-Christians throughout the world.

Our ministry? It revolves around expository preaching, indepth Bible study, way-of-life evangelism, training programs with biblical balance, and orientation for all new members.

My key assistants at Southside Tabernacle are the associate pastor, the Rev. Richard Jackson, and associate ministers, Horace Holloway, Ralph Johnson, and Elix Williams.

Our Lord's Day (Sunday) "opportunities" or services, include the 9:30 A.M. church school, the 10:45 A.M. morning worship, Church Training at 6 P.M., and the evening worship at 7 P.M. The morning service is broadcast live from the sanctuary over Radio Station WRXB of Saint Petersburg.

Our midweek come together is held each Wednesday at 6 P.M., with women of the congregation preparing food for all. No one is charged for the full-course meals.

Special ministries at Southside Tabernacle include our "Design-for-Living Seminars," "Serendipity Forums," "Nouthetic Counseling" and "Ministry of Special Education."

"Design-for-Living Seminars" are planned sessions for couples desiring workable principles to strengthen their marriage and home life. They are conducted on weekends at local or area retreat centers and motels.

"Serendipity Forums" are designed to produce unexpected discoveries arrived at through creative and unhampered discussions on the art of marital communication.

"Nouthetic Counseling" provides advice with direction, deals with business and vocational matters, as well as personal matters, marital problems, and family concerns.

And, ah, our "Ministry of Special Education!" It is one very close to my heart, and deals with filling the spiritual needs of the mentally and emotionally handicapped. The basic spiritual needs of these "special people," I have discovered, are the same as those of all other people. Therefore, we attempt to help them develop.

I am thoroughly convinced that Southside Tabernacle has truly embarked upon a greater dimension of ministry!—A greater dimension of ministry to the metropolis of Pinellas County which has concretized the convictions long held by this writer.

The question/answer essay on race established some of those vital convictions which are tantamount to the Bible believing, practicing congregation.

Race [1]

The proper vein in which to approach such a vital subject is found in that profound statement and text given by the Lord Jesus Christ to those Pharisaic Jews who had rejected him as "The Light of the World" . . . but many believed on him. "If ye continue in my word, then are ye my disciples indeed" (John 8:31). "We . . . were never in bondage to any man." (We never were, are not now, and never will be in bondage to any man.) So they asked, "How sayest thou, Ye shall be made free?" (John 8:33).

However, they made the same mistake that is so widespread today. They failed to discern between a true and a false freedom. I believe that there is a need for genuine freedom that allows one to be honest and open, and freed from some of those concepts which we have about people of different skin pigmentation. What

[1] This paper was prepared for the First Baptist Church (white) of Tampa, Florida, Single Adult Retreat, Saturday, September 19, 1970.

kind of freedom is yours?

In the keynote address to the BWA Eleventh Congress in 1965, Dr. Herschel H. Hobbs said that Charles Kingsley makes a very important distinction for us. "There are two freedoms—the false, where a man is free to do what he likes; the true, where a man is free to do what he ought." In other words, there is the false freedom from outward restraint, and there is the true freedom from inward bondage.

Some conscientious people are sincerely seeking the truth in areas that affect human existence and proper relationship. And without controversy, most of us would readily admit that the racial conflict that confronts this country is tearing it apart.

Miss Hefley has invited me to speak to you from the one word "Race" and discuss some questions with you (because I am not sure that I am able to answer them to your satisfaction).

I was very pleased to discover that the topic is race and not a particular ethnic group, because this gives us the opportunity to look at God's capstone of creation from the proper perspective.

Webster defines race as "any of the three primary divisions of mankind as distinguished especially by color, any geographical, national or tribal ethnic grouping."

What does God have to say in regards to people as a race or ethnic group? He doesn't, because he made man and not a *race.* It is interesting to know that the word race does not appear in God's Word regarding the human family.

In the August 1970, issue of the *Home Mission* magazine, Dr. W. R. Grigg writes, "We need to change our definition of man. To define man in terms of color, race, national origin, or any physical classification is too low an estimate of man and is beneath the Christian teaching that man is a soul made in the likeness of God."

In Acts 10:34, we learn from Peter's experience that God is no "face receiver" or shows no partiality between human persons. Dr. Herschel H. Hobbs wrote in this same vein in the special issue "We hold these truths," session six page 25, "God made man in the dignity of personality. He never violates any man's personality. Anything which does is sinful in God's sight."

"The Judeo-Christian Scriptures teach the universal brotherhood of man's unique relationship to God. The Scriptures which are sacred to both Jews and Christians teach that God created the first man and the first woman in his own image, breathed into their nostrils the breath of life and they became living souls, and all human beings come to procreation from Adam and Eve. The New Testament, so sacred to Christians, declares that the eternal Christ in the fullness of time became incarnated in the person of historic Jesus, is the light which enlightens every anthropos (member of the human race) coming into the cosmos! Too many Christians have been prone to overlook these teachings and their real meaning in all human relations. Yes, all men are brothers in the flesh and blood relationship, whether they ever become brothers 'in Christ' or not. On the basis of God's word, this is the basic promise for human relations. All mankind shares a common humanity." This article appeared in the *Togetherness* of February, 1970, written by the editor, Dr. J. H. Avery.

We will now consider the statement and questions for discussion.

As the socioeconomic level of the Negro (also education) goes up, race color will be minimized as a problem between individuals.

Comment: Possible but not necessarily. Man needs a change of attitude.

Q. What does the Baptist church think of mixed marriages?

A. When it comes to this matter of mixed marriage, most of the Baptists whom I have talked with along these lines are against it. They reason that God never intended this to take place (especially Negro and Caucasian). Therefore, the majority of Baptists (mainly the so-called white) detest the idea with holy fervor. However, an objective examination of the record will reveal that the Bible has no special teachings that can properly be used to support any particular position on mixed marriage. The Jews in the Old Testament were commanded to refrain from mixed marriage. Six or seven nations are listed (Ex. 34:10–16; Deut. 7:1–3). A study of the references will reveal that the restrictions were primarily national and tribal and not racial. In contrast to the opposition to mixed marriage in the Old Testament, some of God's saints, such as Abraham (Gen. 16:3), Joseph (Gen. 41:50), and Moses (Ex. 2:21), married foreign wives. The wives of Abraham and Joseph were Egyptians, descendants of Mizraim. Still later, Moses married a Cushite (Num. 12:1) and Cush was one of the sons of Ham (Gen. 10:6). The word Cush means black and is translated Ethiopia in some places in the Old Testament (see Ps. 68:31; Isa. 18:1).

There may be and are some common sense arguments against mixed marriages but the Bible does not contain a direct, authoritative word for or against mixed marriages. We may and can find some basic principles that will apply but we do not find a specific enough position regarding mixed marriage to be dogmatic about what the Bible teaches.

Q. Have the churches accepted desegregation very fast, easily, or have they rejected it within their congregation?

A. The churches have been the slowest. The reason seems to lie in the fact that churches don't know who they are, and don't know what to do. Therefore, out of fear, desegregation is rejected. Of course, I don't see how churches can be a New Testament church which is people with "whosoever will come, let him come." In other words, the (body) church of Christ is integrated! The rejection of desegregation on the part of the congregation is based on their relationship to Christ, for "There is neither Jew nor Greek, . . . there is neither male nor female: for ye are all one in Christ Jesus" (Gal. 3:28).

Q. What are some of the best ways to improve race relations on a national scale and at a local level?

A. Following the Detroit riot in the summer of 1967, a Negro minister was asked to explain it. He said, "I don't know. I guess the black man learned to hate before the white man learned to love." There is no substitute for love because "God is love." Love is the basis.

Love is patient and kind; love is not jealous, or conceited, or proud; love is not ill-mannered, . . . or irritable; love does not keep a record of wrongs; love is not happy with evil, but is happy with truth, love never gives up, its faith, hope and patience never fail. Love is eternal (1 Cor. 13:4–8, TEV).

Q. Do you feel the Baptist church should be integrated?

A. Yes, if heaven is integrated.

Q. Do you believe in interracial marriages?

A. It is not what I believe about it. However, I am for what God is for and against what he's against. Therefore, when love is involved, and God's will is at stake—who am I to say who is to marry whom?

The Word says:

Be ye not unequally yoked together with unbelievers: for what fellowship hath righteousness with unrighteousness: and what communion hath light with darkness or what part hath he that believeth with an infidel?

Q. Do the Negroes blame this generation of other races for the slavery of their forefathers?

A. Yes, the masses do. But those who have been set free by God's redeeming grace are so secured in Christ until we do not have time to live in the past, because being in Christ gives one a true and untarnished dignity.

Q. What type of help does the black community want from the whites?

A. It is not necessarily help that is wanted, but rather a true demonstration of these words, "One Nation Under God, Indivisible, with Liberty and Justice for All." (See 1 John 4:17–21.)

Epilogue

As this book was prepared for publication in January of 1977, two churches in Saint Petersburg continued to experience the joy and affirmation of being a part of something God wanted to do in their city. Both Southside Tabernacle Baptist Church and First Baptist Church bear a stronger witness in the city because of a willingness to pursue an unusual approach to a not so unusual problem. Each fellowship ministers with a new boldness and openness because of the experience of victory over age-old barriers of misunderstanding. Fellowship in the truest sense of the New Testament concept became more of a reality as black and white Baptists discovered a new way in which they could cooperate in an endeavor to enrich the kingdom of God.

Three pastors share a deep appreciation and affection for one another. A mutual respect for the problems and abilities of the others has enabled them to grow in their understanding of the broader ministry to which God has called them. No small part of the consequences of the merger was the friendship developed among these three men.